ONE-MINUTE
TIPS FOR
CONFIDENT
COMMUNICATION

Other Books by Mike Bechtle

It's Better to Bite Your Tongue Than Eat Your Words

The People Pleaser's Guide to Loving Others without Losing Yourself

Dealing with the Elephant in the Room

What Was He Thinking?

People Can't Drive You Crazy If You Don't Give Them the Keys

How to Communicate with Confidence

Evangelism for the Rest of Us

ONE-MINUTE TIPS FOR CONFIDENT COMMUNICATION

DR. MIKE BECHTLE

SPIRE

© 2022 by Mike Bechtle

Published by Revell
a division of Baker Publishing Group
PO Box 6287, Grand Rapids, MI 49516-6287
www.revellbooks.com

Material adapted from *How to Communicate with Confidence*, published by Spire in 2013, originally published under the title *Confident Conversation* by Revell in 2008.

Printed in the United States of America

Library of Congress Cataloging-in-Publication Data
Names: Bechtle, Mike, 1952– author.
Title: One-minute tips for confident communication / Dr. Mike Bechtle.
Description: Grand Rapids, MI : Revell, a division of Baker Publishing
  Group, [2022] | Includes bibliographical references.
Identifiers: LCCN 2022001728 | ISBN 9780800742164 (trade paperback) |
  ISBN 9781493438860 (ebook)
Subjects: LCSH: Interpersonal communication—Miscellanea. |
  Conversation—Miscellanea. | Life skills—Miscellanea.
Classification: LCC BF637.C45 B4296 2022 | DDC 153.6—dc23/
  eng/20220406
LC record available at https://lccn.loc.gov/2022001728

Baker Publishing Group publications use paper produced from sustainable forestry practices and post-consumer waste whenever possible.

23   24   25   26   27   28   8   7   6   5   4

To Marco

God has given you an amazing gift of conversation.
I'm so grateful that I get to experience it so often.
I can't wait to see how He will use you to impact the world!

CONTENTS

Starting a Conversation 47

Continuing a Conversation   59

Ending a Conversation   73

The Power of Listening   87

Contents

Rethinking Stress   97

Curiosity: Your Never-Ending Vault of Topics   103

Tough Conversations   117

Attitude   125

High-Tech Talking 131

Fine-Tuning Your Skills 137

INTRODUCTION

You probably picked up this book because of the word *confident* in the title. You've had a lot of experience having conversations—some of which went well and some that didn't. Unfortunately, you never seem to know which way they're going to go.

Wouldn't it be great to enter every conversation with confidence? You'd know what to say, what not to say, and how to be fully engaged in the dialogue. You'd know how to start a conversation, keep it going, and end it well. You would have mastered the basic skills that make every conversation effective, whether you're talking to an introvert or an extrovert—and you would have overcome the self-defeating thoughts that get in the way. Most of all, you wouldn't have to become something you're not; you'd get to be *you*!

That's the promise of this book: You'll be able to communicate with confidence in *any* situation.

Read this book completely through to get a sense of how all the tips fit together. Then go back and focus on one tip each day, looking for opportunities to try them out in real relationships. There's no rush; in fact, you'll find the greatest impact by applying each one and mastering it before moving on to the next.

Welcome to the journey!

UNIQUENESS: THE KEY RESOURCE FOR CONFIDENCE

1. You can learn to communicate more effectively.

Conversation is one of the basic tools for twenty-first-century living. Almost everything we do depends on it. We can't buy a car, negotiate a business deal, or strengthen a relationship without conversation. When it's done effectively, we get satisfying results. When it's done ineffectively, we feel dissatisfied with the outcome.

But we don't spend a lot of time trying to improve how we communicate. We'll pay someone to help us improve our tennis game, learn photography, or develop our computer skills. But when it comes to making conversation, we rarely make a conscious effort to develop a skill that can have a huge impact on how well we live each day.

No matter what your personality style, you can make conversing one of the most rewarding and positive things you do in life. Since you really don't have a choice (you have to make conversation to make it through life), you have every motivation to take the steps to get really good at it. By consciously working on your skills, you'll be able to enjoy connections you already have and look forward to new conversations. You can build your skills at a safe, comfortable speed, using methods that fit your style and moving into new skill levels when you've mastered the current ones.

2. Embrace your personality as your superpower.

You might feel that your personality style holds you back in conversations. Maybe you've read a book or article on communication but found tips that seemed foreign to you. Discouraged, you resigned yourself to making the best of a bad situation.

But the problem isn't your personality type. The problem comes when we try to change who we are to become something we're not. Instead of compensating for a perceived weakness, we can embrace our personality and explore ways to capitalize on it. Taking golf lessons doesn't change your body type; it teaches you to get the most out of the body you have. Why not spend time studying your personality and learning to get the most out of it? The benefits will take you a lot farther than simply improving your putting skills.

3. Your uniqueness is your most valuable asset.

My wife and I visited a small art gallery by the beach a few years ago. We saw one picture that looked like a checkerboard made up of pastel construction paper cut into squares. It was mounted on a canvas and suspended in a glass case. It was interesting and seemed well done. But then my eyes caught the price tag: $250,000. Not being art connoisseurs, we asked the manager what it was about a piece of art that could make it worth a quarter of a million dollars. He simply pointed to the signature at the bottom. We didn't recognize the name, but he assured us that anyone in the art community would recognize it in an instant.

The value came from the creator. People will pay more for an original than for a copy of the same piece. That uniqueness that sets it apart from everything else.

We humans almost always seem dissatisfied with who we are. If we have straight hair, we wish it were curly. If we have curly hair, we pay to have it straightened. We're always too something or not enough something else.

Quiet people think everyone else is more outgoing and knows how to strike up a conversation easily and keep it going. Deep inside, they feel like there's something wrong with them. They believe that others notice how uncomfortable they are in conversation, as if they are wearing a sign around their neck that says, "Don't ask me about my day."

So introverts try to *act* like extroverts. They *pretend* to be more outgoing so they can fit in but find it draining to keep pretending to be something they aren't. They read tips about how to be more outgoing, but it keeps them from dealing with the real issue.

The solution is to realize that our personality isn't a mistake; it's who we are. If we learn how to capitalize on the personality we have, we can stop pretending. The best way to become a world-class conversationalist is to accept who we are and build on that honest foundation.

4. Confidence happens one step at a time.

Many of us walk into a social gathering assuming we're the most uncomfortable person in the room. We feel like we're the lone struggler in a room full of confident communicators. In reality, many of the people in the room are thinking the same thing.

I often assume that the confidence I see in everyone else is what they're actually feeling. But I realize that I frequently try to give off an air of confidence with others even when I'm not feeling that way. If that's what I'm doing, it's realistic to assume that others are doing it too. Imagine what it would be like if everyone said aloud what their emotions were during each conversation:

- "I'm afraid to talk to you because I'm afraid you won't like me."
- "I'm really intimidated by you."
- "I'm a lot more interested in what I have to say than in what you think."

There's a better way—and you won't have to act confident. You'll *be* confident.

Getting from where we are now to a place of conversational confidence might seem like a huge task. But if we break it into small steps and measure our progress, we'll be amazed at how much "ground" we can cover over time. Small steps taken consistently yield big results.

Learning to converse confidently may seem as if it involves a steep learning curve. But if we plan carefully and take the process step-by-step, using persistence and patience, we'll achieve our goal. Measuring our progress is important, because otherwise we'll just be looking at how much distance remains to reach our goal. But it's important to see how far we've come.

The best place to start is to realize that you don't have to become something you're not. Instead, you want to:

- Recognize your temperament and personality.
- Accept the uniqueness of that personality.
- Develop your personality, using it as the basis for how you interact with others.

It's a matter of working from our strengths. Learning to make conversation will become a realistic goal when we follow a carefully designed process using sequential steps, one at a time. The smaller the steps and the more time we take practicing them and making them part of our lives, the easier the process will be—and the more confident we'll become.

5. Learn to value the differences of others.

Paula loves a good party. She thought that surprising Jenn on her birthday with a big celebration would be a perfect way to demonstrate her friendship. When Jenn's response was cordial but unenthusiastic, Paula felt hurt and unappreciated.

Phil spent the weekend attending a wedding, having dinner with a group from church, and participating in Sunday activities with extended family. A friend suggested that Phil and his new wife, Barb, join them for coffee on Monday night with several couples. He was looking forward to spending a quiet evening at home, so he politely declined. After renting a movie and buying Chinese take-out, he couldn't understand Barb's disappointment when she found out about the invitation.

Paula and Barb love being surrounded by other people and assume that everyone else does too. Jenn and Phil don't mind being around people, but it drains their emotional tanks pretty quickly.

Both preferences are real. Neither of them is something that needs to be fixed; they simply describe what each person prefers. Ignoring that uniqueness in others puts up a barrier that makes effective communication difficult at best and often impossible.

THE POWER OF EMPATHY

6. Learn to accept others exactly the way they are.

There are two foundational realities that make conversation effective:

1. Understanding and accepting who you really are
2. Understanding and accepting who the other person is

Understanding and accepting ourselves means we don't compare ourselves to others. Comparison is one of the greatest hindrances to good conversation. It puts the focus on us and how we perform instead of mining the richness of another person's life and experience. We end up trying to shape how others see us, and we end up being a counterfeit version of who we really are. It's tough to have a real relationship when we're pretending.

Understanding and accepting others happens when we don't do "reverse comparison," where we evaluate others using ourselves as the standard. It means we become intentional about listening to their perspectives, listening to understand instead of trying to convince them that our ideas are right (and theirs are wrong). It's not about agreeing or disagreeing, because relationships aren't built on thinking the same way. They're built on mutual respect for each other as people, not for our positions.

Having that perspective will eliminate a large percentage of the conversational issues we face because we'll be communicating with integrity instead of playing games to impress each other.

7. Look at others through their filters.

Let's say I have an idea in my head that I want to express to you. My goal is for you to know exactly what I'm thinking. Wouldn't it be nice if we could transfer the information digitally so it would arrive in your head in exactly the same form it was in my head?

Since that's not an option, I have to use another method: words. They can be spoken or written, but humans use words to connect with each other. So I select the words that best express what I'm thinking, and you receive those words. Sound good so far?

The problem is the meaning we both give to the same words. The words I choose come through a series of filters, such as:

- Language
- Background
- Education
- Socioeconomic status
- Culture

So what one sees as neutral words might be packed with meaning for the other person. When you hear those words, you have your own series of filters to interpret them. I might mean one thing, but you hear the same words and get a totally different idea.

For example, I might say "It's hot today." I grew up in the Phoenix desert, so "hot" means something totally different to me than it does to a person from Alaska. Residents of Georgia have still another filter (a humid one) to interpret their concept of heat.

With all those filters, it's amazing that we manage to communicate at all! Looking at the same words through different filters creates barriers to effective conversation. Knowing that those filters exist can go a long way toward building mutual understanding.

8. Don't let filters become barriers.

Is there a food you don't like—that you've never tasted? Even though you haven't tried it, you're convinced that it doesn't taste good. Maybe it's a certain kind of vegetable or an exotic meat. You just know intuitively that you won't like it, and you have no intention of testing your theory.

For me, it's sushi. I haven't tried it, but I'm convinced that it's not good. I grew up around sushi in Arizona, but we called it bait. I don't eat bait.

The things we believe determine what we do. If we believe a certain food isn't good, we don't eat it. That belief might be right or wrong, but it can become a filter that determines our actions. Those actions produce results. When we don't like the results we're getting, it means that our filters have produced barriers to getting the results we want.

Linda becomes the new manager of a department, and the exiting manager tells her that all the people on the team are incompetent. When Linda steps into the new job, she sees her people through that filter, assuming that they're incompetent. So what does she do? She starts micromanaging them. What results do you get when people are micromanaged? Disloyalty, frustration, and poor performance.

Linda sees the poor performance and assumes the filter is correct: Her people are incompetent. So she micromanages even more, causing a downward spiral of resentment. Her filter has become a barrier to managing her people effectively.

Instead of increasing her micromanagement, what if Linda challenged her filter? She could say, "These people might have been incompetent in the past, but they might become more competent if someone believed in them and encouraged them." With that new filter, she would remove the barrier. Her actions would reflect that belief, and she would affirm their skills and strengths. The results of that encouragement could be a stronger team with continually improving performance.

Our success in making conversation depends on whether or not our filters become barriers.

9. Don't worry about who's right or wrong; go for understanding.

Sometimes when we think we're right and the other person is wrong, we feel an obligation to correct them and get them to see things our way. That's a dangerous perspective. True exploring isn't for the purpose of changing someone's mind; it's for understanding them.

My wife, Diane, is a doer. When she starts something, she finishes as quickly and thoroughly as possible. In meetings, she will listen for a while and then ask, "OK, what are we going to do, and who's going to be responsible?"

I'm a thinker. I'm usually seen as an idea person. Give me a problem, and I'll come up with six different possible solutions. I'll come up with things nobody else thinks of. I never actually *do* anything though; I just dream about doing things.

Shortly after we were married, our different approaches became an issue for us. I thought Diane worked too hard at things and needed to lighten up. On the other hand, it was tough for her to see me brainstorm great ideas but never take any action.

Gradually, we came to understand that neither approach was best, just different. We learned to focus on the issue instead of seeing each other as the problem. The more we worked to understand each other's perspectives, the easier it was to draw from those differences to come up with strong, creative solutions. The more we've explored those perspectives over the years, the stronger our relationship has become.

BUILDING YOUR CONVERSATION SKILLS

10. Avoid tips and tricks that don't fit your temperament.

If your experience with books or seminars on conversation has been awkward or ineffective in the past, you might not be very excited about more tips and techniques. You feel the need strongly enough to read this book, but you're worried that you'll have to stretch too far outside your comfort zone to make it a reality. Or you're thinking that the techniques might help, but they will always be uncomfortable.

The bad news is that you're right—about the tips and techniques. If you simply pick random ideas that are foreign to you and force them into your conversations, the process will continue to be painful. The good news is that when you select techniques and tips that match your temperament and personality, you've removed that barrier, and you will find conversing with others to be exciting, fulfilling, and fun. That's the goal—to provide customized tools to help you enjoy the process of communication.

Negative experiences leave us with three options:

1. Avoid making conversation with people.
2. Make conversation but do it poorly and painfully.
3. Analyze our unique personality and learn skills to connect well with others.

You may have lived with the first two for a long time. Now it's time to use the third one to remove barriers and gain new skills for effective communication.

11. Find conversational skills that work for introverts (if that's you).

Instead of grabbing every idea you hear about how to be a good conversationalist, be selective. Ask yourself, "Does this sound like an idea that I'd feel comfortable with?" Keep it if it does and ignore it if it doesn't.

Here are examples that might work for an introvert:

- Don't feel pressured to give an immediate reply. Just say, "That's an interesting perspective. I need to think about that a bit. I'll let you know my response tomorrow."

- Learn simple ways to end a conversation when you feel it's time. (You'll learn those later in this book.)
- Writing is a way to clarify your thoughts, so don't be afraid to put together an email with your ideas. Even if you don't send it, you'll have more clarity when you present your ideas in person.

12. Find conversational skills that work for extroverts (if that's you).

If you're an extrovert, it's easy to assume that being comfortable in conversations is the same as being effective. Don't overlook techniques that might allow you to draw out the best contribution from others, such as:

- Don't immediately share every idea that comes to mind. It might feel like you're just being helpful, but others might feel like they don't have space to contribute.
- In a group setting, share one idea—then wait until three others have shared before jumping in again.
- In a one-on-one setting, listen to what the other person says, and ask a clarifying question or two before adding more of your own thoughts.

13. Change your self-talk.

When we don't have complete information, it's easy to make assumptions about what the other person is thinking. Unfortunately, once we've made those assumptions, we've also decided that they're true. Then we act on the basis of what we believe is true, even if it isn't.

We tell ourselves things like:

- "They're confident in this conversation, and I'm not."
- "If this conversation is going to work, I have to make them like me."
- "I have to be in control of where this conversation goes."
- "I'm too quiet to make this conversation work."
- "I have to be prepared with lots of conversational topics."

When these barriers characterize our self-talk, we set ourselves up for failure. We believe what we're telling ourselves and then act on those assumptions. The key is to recognize what we're telling ourselves and then rewrite each assumption into one that's more accurate.

Here are some possible "rewrites" of the above barriers:

Old: "They're confident in this conversation, and I'm not."

New: "I really don't know what they're thinking; they might not be as comfortable as they appear on the surface."

Old: "If this conversation is going to work, I have to make them like me."

New: "I'm not responsible for how the other person feels about me; I just have to be myself."

Old: "I have to be in control of where this conversation goes."
New: "Both of us are responsible for where this conversation goes."

Old: "I'm too quiet to make this conversation work."
New: "I can learn skills to converse effectively based on my own personality."

Old: "I have to be prepared with lots of conversational topics."
New: "I need to be a good listener to pick up on things to talk about."

14. Take responsibility for yourself—only.

When my wife and I went through premarital counseling, we were reminded that it's never accurate to say, "You make me so angry." Anger is a choice that we make. I can say or do something that my wife might respond to in anger—but she can also choose a different response. I'm only responsible for my choices, not another person's reactions.

In conversation, I can only take care of myself. I can't make another person like me, but I can be myself. If that person doesn't respond the way I'd like them to, it doesn't mean I'm a bad person. It simply means that they are choosing to respond that way, and it's out of my control. The more I try to control the other person, the more frustrated I'll become.

I can only take care of me; that's my responsibility. You can only take care of you.

15. You're only responsible for what you bring to a conversation, not the outcome.

There are no guarantees that every conversation will be effective and comfortable. But when a conversation doesn't go well, you can't assume responsibility for its failure. Just as it takes two or more people to hold a conversation, it takes those same people to determine the outcome. Assuming that you hold the total responsibility for the "success" of a conversation ignores the reality of the other person's communication skills. Everything they do in that conversation contributes to the outcome but doesn't determine it—which is true for you as well.

It's like playing chess. You might have different skill levels at playing, but neither player is totally responsible for the outcome. No one knows what moves they are going to make at the beginning of the game since those decisions will be based on what the other player does. It's a dynamic process, with both players using the best of their skills to make an enjoyable game.

There is a difference, however, between chess and conversation. In chess, there will be a winner and a loser. In conversation, the goal is for both people to win.

16. You don't have to know everything about everything.

Explorers go into the wilderness without knowing what they'll find. They would probably feel more secure if they brought supplies for every possible situation, but they would be too loaded down to make the trip. So they bring the tools essential for survival: a compass, water, maps, matches, and other resources to handle the situations they might encounter. They make sure they know well how to use the tools before beginning the trip.

It's overwhelming to enter a conversation thinking we need to know everything about everything just in case it comes up. But if we can discern what tools are essential for communication, we can gain confidence to embark on the adventure. We don't need every tool there is; we just need to become proficient with the best tools—the ones that "fit" our personality.

Here are some tools you'll need for exploration:

- *Mindset:* A healthy perspective on yourself (no comparison), a realistic perspective on the other person (no need to change them), and deep curiosity (quest for discovery).
- *Skillset:* Mastery of the tools and techniques you're learning in this book and a willingness to accept imperfection as you grow your skills.
- *Toolset:* A variety of resources you have collected over time that help you connect with others.

17. You can't rush growth.

We don't become seasoned explorers overnight. We start slowly, using our new tools to venture into new areas. Over time, we gain confidence, which allows us to grow into deeper levels of comfort in conversations.

When our kids were little, they learned to ride a bike. At first, they had training wheels. They were scared but became quite proficient at making circles around the driveway. Gradually, they developed a sense of balance, and the training wheels came off. But that didn't mean we sent them on errands five miles away. They stayed in the driveway as their confidence grew. Then their range expanded to the sidewalk between our house and the neighbor's driveway. They learned to watch for cars and how to spot other hazards. It was a big day when we finally allowed them to go around the block by themselves.

They don't ride their bikes much anymore. But those basic skills turned into the ability to drive a car. They've become comfortable with the skills of finding their way around a city, and they experience the freedom that comes from knowing how to use those skills.

Learn how to become a skilled explorer. For an introvert, taking on that role will be the key to gaining the confidence needed to excel in making conversation. For an extrovert, it will provide the tools to make conversations more effective than they've ever been in the past.

18. Learn the three approaches to a conversation.

This diagram represents three approaches to a conversation:

1. *Focusing on the left circle.*

    Most people who want to improve their communication skills focus on the left circle. They read books and articles, trying to make their circle bigger. It's a great way to develop a bigger library of topics to discuss. But if they focus solely on the left circle, they'll miss one of the greatest resources to make a conversation work: the experience and perspective of the other person.

2. *Focusing on the right circle.*

    Rick Warren begins *The Purpose Driven Life* by saying, "It's not about you."[1] That perspective opens the door for an effective conversation. Most people spend their energy trying to say the right thing in the right way and in the right sequence to get the desired response. But if we only focus on what *we* say, we're missing key elements of the conversation: what the *other person* is thinking, feeling, and saying.

This approach recognizes the value of another person's perspective. Exploring another person's experience provides a collection of ingredients that can make a conversation move in new and exciting directions.

But strictly focusing on the perspective of others also fosters a one-sided relationship. And it doesn't help with how to get a conversation started. A third approach makes it easy for anyone to make conversation connections.

3. *Focusing on the common ground.*

The key to good conversation is to explore the overlap—the common ground where the two circles come together.

That overlap may be tiny or surprisingly large, but it's the place to begin a conversation. We don't have to become something we're not; we simply have to figure out the common language that both of us speak. As we begin conversing in that area of common experience and interest, we build a foundation for exploring the "unknown edges" of each other's circles. It moves our perspective from "me" to "you" to "us."

COMMON GROUND: THE KEY INGREDIENT FOR CONFIDENCE

19. Finding common ground makes it easy to start a conversation.

It's tempting to focus our energy on having a lot of interesting things to talk about. An easier way is to explore another person's experience, then mix it with your own to find things that overlap. That common ground is where genuine connection begins in a new conversation. You don't have to be clever or well-spoken; you just have to be intentional about finding the areas of interest you both share.

Take one topic and explore further, and it will lead you to other areas of mutual interest or experience. It's an ever-widening circle that can grow as the conversation progresses. The process frees both people from having to think of things to talk about because interesting topics rise to the surface.

Searching for common ground is like pushing a car. It gets the conversation in motion, which builds momentum for future conversations.

20. Exploring differences keeps a conversation moving forward.

Common ground is a catalyst for starting a relationship. Once that relationship is in motion, it's time to move beyond those similarities. If all we do is stick with common ground, conversation will be like talking to ourselves. Once a conversation is in motion, the differences build momentum and keep it going.

The more differences there are between people, the more ingredients that can be added to the conversation. Those differences provide new topics to explore, which makes it easier to take the conversation in new directions. You don't have to become a library of conversational topics, because that would make you solely responsible for what you talk about. Just learn the skills of exploration, discovering the differences between you and the other person, and then use natural curiosity to build energy in the conversation.

It's a whole lot easier than having to always think of what to say next.

21. Find common ground in shared experiences.

We moved recently, and we haven't met our new neighbors yet. Their work hours are different from ours, so we haven't happened to be in our driveways at the same time. My wife, Diane, baked some cookies for Christmas, put them in a bag, and added a card. We rang the doorbells of the houses around us, but no one answered. So we hung the bags on our neighbors' doorknobs, hoping to find common ground (everyone has to eat).

A few days later, we found a bag of chocolate truffles hanging from our doorknob with a handmade card from one of the neighbors. The next day, the college-age son of another neighbor came by to deliver a box of candy from his parents. They evidently speak mostly Chinese and sent him to make the contact. Even though we still haven't had a formal conversation, we connected through the common language of caring.

How do you find that common ground? Simply look for it. Everyone is human, which means they share a number of life experiences and emotions. Those similarities can be the touch points that connect people at the heart.

If it's a neighbor, ask about something happening on your block: "I'm noticing that the roots of those trees the city planted are pulling up the sidewalks in front of my house. Is that happening to you too?"

At work, think of a noncontroversial issue that everyone might share: "Somebody told me we can bring our lunch and put it in the fridge in the break room. At my old company, it would often get stolen. Does that happen here, or do you think it will be safe?"

At a social event, ask a simple question: "So how do you know the host?"

Finding common ground is easy if you're attentive. Just look for things you find interesting in the environment and see if others feel the same.

22. Recognize the benefits of common ground.

Explorers begin in an area they're familiar with and gradually move into new areas. They're keenly aware of their surroundings, observing new sights and sounds and processing them against what they already know. Their current knowledge expands as they make those new observations.

We enter every conversation with our current background and experience, and the other person does the same. When we explore areas we both have in common, it sets the conversation in motion. From there, we expand the conversation when we look for each other's unique perspectives and experiences.

Focusing on common ground provides a number of specific benefits to effective communication:

It gives you more to talk about. When you feel like the only one who needs to contribute to a conversation, you have a limited number of ingredients to add to the recipe. But looking through another person's perspective is like looking through their kitchen cupboards. They'll have things in their cupboards that you don't, which means you have the potential for preparing dishes you couldn't have imagined before.

It takes the pressure off. When we look through only our own perspective, we wonder how we are coming across to the other person. But when we attempt to see things through their perspective, we can relax. Genuine interest in others takes energy, which means that energy isn't as available for focusing on ourselves.

It adds adventure. Quiet personalities often associate words like *terror* and *panic* with making conversation, not *excitement* and *adventure*. But by using a simple process that's based on what both people bring to a conversation, the encounter can be something they look forward to. Learning the unique experiences of another person can be like traveling to a new country. You may be entering unfamiliar territory, but there's a sense of anticipation because there's so much to see and learn. Once you go, you want to go back.

It takes the guesswork out of a relationship. Most new relationships are characterized by playing games. We listen to people's words, watch their expressions and gestures, hear their tone of voice, and make assumptions about what they're thinking. But often, we're wrong. Learning to gain another person's perspective provides accurate processing of these conversational dynamics. We don't have to guess what their motives are; we can simply talk about them openly and without defensiveness.

23. Prepare for any conversation.

Backpackers sit on a mountain peak and study a map to determine where they're headed. They scan the landscape, look for landmarks, and identify the direction they need to go. To get to the next peak, however, they have to go through a forested valley where the landmarks aren't visible. Once they've entered the forest, they pull out the compass and follow the route they've already planned.

Too often we go into a conversation without planning and wonder why it doesn't go well. Preparation for a social encounter is like studying a map before beginning the journey. It gives you a sense of where you're heading. Based on that preparation, you'll come up with specific ideas to keep you on track as the conversation progresses. Those are your compass; they keep you moving in the right direction.

How do you prepare for a conversation? By focusing on three things: you, the other person, and the situation you'll be encountering.

You: Be ready when someone says, "So tell me about you." Develop two "elevator speeches." One should be a thirty-second description of who you are and what you do. The other should do the same thing without mentioning your employment. You'll use the first one often, since people will often begin a conversation by asking, "So what do you do?" But the second can open up whole new areas of conversational exploration.

The other person: A typical opening question is "What do you do?" We assume it's a good question to find areas of common ground. But it has some inherent risks. The conversation might stay one-dimensional, or the person might drone on endlessly about a technical job that is totally foreign to you. If they're recently unemployed or in a negative job situation, you might create an uncomfortable moment that's hard to recover from.

Try asking questions that have nothing to do with their career. Think about questions you would feel comfortable answering about yourself.

The situation: A good conversation has a balance of input from both parties. Focusing on either you or the other person risks an imbalance. That's why it's generally safest to focus your comments or questions on either the current situation or outside events that might interest both of you.

STARTING A CONVERSATION

24. Don't let assumptions stop a conversation before it starts.

When a space shuttle launches, it burns 90 percent of its fuel in the first few minutes to escape the earth's gravity. From that point forward, the fuel consumption drops to a fraction of that original amount.

For many people, starting a conversation is the hardest part of communication. It seems to take 90 percent of our energy just to make the initial contact because:

- We don't know how to initiate the interaction.
- We don't know what to say first.
- We don't know if the other person wants to talk to us.
- We don't know how to approach someone.

But once the conversation has started, maintaining the momentum is easier than getting it going in the first place.

An effective conversation begins before the first word is spoken. Both parties go through an unconscious dialogue in their own minds about the accessibility of the other person. We read a person's body language and facial expressions and interpret those signals to determine the chances for success in approaching them. If we assume the signals are positive, we proceed, cautiously measuring their responses. If we decide the signals are negative, we assume they won't be interested.

But often those assumptions are inaccurate. It's important to separate what we observe from our interpretation of those observations.

25. Don't assume your first impressions are true.

While teaching a seminar a few years ago, I observed an older participant in the front row who was obviously disinterested. He would sigh loudly during the class, roll his eyes occasionally, and make no eye contact. His body language and facial expressions seemed to indicate that he would rather be anywhere than in that classroom. I assumed that he had been forced to attend by his manager.

But at the end of the class, he approached me and shook my hand. With no facial expression, he said, "Thank you. Best class I've ever attended. Changed my life."

I thought he was joking. But then he continued: "I'm in charge of accounting for this company worldwide. I'm bringing forty-five accountants to Tulsa for a conference in a couple of months. Would you come do this seminar for them?"

Since that time, I've learned to be a little less certain about my assumptions. If a person has his arms crossed, I could assume he's closed and resistant. Sometimes he's just cold.

26. Make the first move.

There are two ways to initiate a conversation:

1. Wait for someone to approach you.
2. Approach someone.

The first approach is more common for introverts. They don't want to risk rejection or appear foolish, so they wait for someone to approach. If the other person takes the initiative, the introvert assumes that they find enough interest in them to strike up a conversation. But this approach has some inherent problems:

- If no one approaches them, it reinforces their feelings of inadequacy.
- It puts the focus on themselves instead of the other person.
- They have no control over the outcome.
- It makes the whole process potentially painful.

The second approach is more common for extroverts. They're not as concerned about how they're being perceived, so they are quick to approach others. They assume that everyone is as comfortable in conversation as they are. When it comes to starting a conversation, it's an effective approach.

Quiet people might find the second approach more threatening, so they don't consider it. But the perceived pain usually comes from assuming what the other person is thinking.

We might assume that if we approach someone, they will be offended. But think about the times you've been approached by someone else. How many times were you offended? In most cases, you were probably grateful that they took the initiative so you didn't have to. If they're standing alone, there's a great chance that they'll welcome the opportunity to talk. The worst that can happen is that there's no chemistry, and you can graciously end that conversation and move to someone else. But that's not usually what happens.

27. Assume that others think you're interesting.

Check your self-talk. If we see ourselves as boring, we assume that others are thinking, *Oh great. Look who I'm getting stuck with.* If we see ourselves as interesting, we assume that they're thinking, *This will be a fun conversation because they're so outgoing.*

We see ourselves in a certain way, and we tend to believe that it's an accurate perception. After all, nobody knows us as well as we do, right? So we assume that those perceptions about ourselves are always accurate and that others must be seeing us in the same way. If we feel positive about ourselves, we think others feel that way too. If we feel negative and critical of ourselves, that must be how others see us.

It's true that we form a quick impression when someone approaches us, but the first few seconds of the conversation tell us if we're correct or not. In the same way, most people give the benefit of the doubt as the conversation begins. They assume that someone approaching them is interesting until they prove otherwise.

You're different from everyone else, which means you're interesting. Give others the chance to discover that for themselves.

28. Be willing to break the ice for others.

We all crave connections. By approaching another person, we're speaking directly to that need. They want conversations to work as much as we do and understand the energy it takes to interact.

Sometimes we assume someone is standing alone because they see themselves as above us. But that's usually not the case. If it were true, they would have stayed home. They're probably waiting for someone to approach them. If you take the initiative, they'll be relieved.

How will you know what to talk about? You won't, but that's one of the biggest advantages you have. It lets you off the hook from needing to have lots of topics to discuss. Start exploring, get the momentum going, and then begin searching for ideas in that new territory.

29. Initiate conversations, and you get to pick who you spend time with.

There's often a fear that if you take the initiative to approach someone and the conversation doesn't go well, you've failed. But that puts all the responsibility on you for a good conversation. Not every interaction has to be great. As you begin to make connections with a variety of people, you'll connect more with some than others. Some connections will be brief and stay on the surface, while others will be extended and dive deeply into each other's lives.

The purpose of conversation isn't to show people how clever you are; it's to make a connection between two people. Not only does the outcome of a conversation say something about you and your conversational skills; it reveals something about the other person as well. It's important to be realistic in how we interpret the results of our interactions.

In a practical sense, here's the greatest advantage of being the one to initiate a conversation: *You get to pick the people you spend time with.*

30. It's easier to join a conversation with a group who's already talking than to start one with an individual.

Years ago, I spent time as a radio announcer. One of the best pieces of advice I received from a mentor was that people don't listen to the radio in groups. They listen by themselves in their cars or at home. If I was going to be successful on the air, I had to hold a conversation with an individual.

So, when you're initiating a conversation, should you start with a group or an individual?

Either one will work. Your ultimate goal is to make a connection with an individual. But approaching a group can be a safe way to make that first contact. Since they're already talking to each other, there's less of a chance that they'll notice you standing alone. So you can "sneak up" on the group and make some observations before deciding to join them.

Grab some snacks and stand close to the group for a couple of minutes. Watch their body language and listen to what they're discussing. The level of their conversation will tell you if this is a group of people who know each other well or if they've just met each other. A group of close friends might form a tight circle to keep intruders away, and they'll discuss issues that have significance only to them. But if they're having a casual conversation about something you have some interest in, stand close enough that people notice your presence. Then say, "Sorry to interrupt, but I heard you talking about XYZ—and that's something I'm really interested in. Would you mind if I join you?"

31. Share your name when connecting with someone you've met before; it takes the pressure off if they've forgotten.

You're at a social event and see someone you recognize and want to connect with. Walk up to them and say, "Hi,

Terry. Dean Smith. We met in Dallas a few months ago, and I just wanted to say hi." At that point, Terry will be relieved, because he might not have remembered your name. You've made it easy for him, and he'll probably respond by introducing you to the group he's talking to—which opens the door to another connection.

If you forget someone else's name when they greet you, don't pretend to remember it. Just say, "Tell me your name again . . . ?" You'll both be more comfortable, and asking demonstrates your integrity. You've shown confidence by not being afraid to admit that you're human.

32. When joining a group conversation, don't do this.

When we don't know what to say first, it's natural to go to things we're most familiar with: ourselves, our opinions, and our experiences. It's comfortable territory, so it seems like a logical place to start. But when others don't know us, it comes across as self-serving and arrogant.

How do you feel when someone talks only about themselves and shows no interest in you? In most cases, you'll end the conversation quickly and move on. But if they show a genuine interest in you, you're inclined to continue. It's not selfish; it's human nature. We're looking for relationships that are mutually beneficial.

That's why focusing on the other person early in the conversation is the best place to start. It's not a gimmick to get them to like you but a genuine expression of care that opens the door to connection.

Explore who they are as a whole person. Don't start by asking about their opinions on volatile issues; it steers the conversation away from who they really are to what beliefs they hold. Once you've solidified that initial contact, you can gradually explore deeper issues—but not at the beginning.

33. When joining a group conversation, do this.

Once you've made your initial entry into a group, what should you say first?

Remember: Your goal is to find common ground. When entering a group, trying to take over the conversation or introduce new topics is not wise. It's safer to pick up on something you've already heard them talking about and make a quick comment or two about it. Comment on something from their perspective rather than your own.

As you enter a group, you hear them discussing the price of gasoline. Don't start by saying, "Well, it's fifty cents higher than that in my neighborhood." Instead, say, "That's a great price. Where do you buy your gas?" If the conversation focuses on the weather, don't start by telling them about the hottest place you've ever lived. Listen long enough to find out what area they're talking about and ask, "Are all of you from that area?" You're raising the flag about your thoughts and quickly lowering it, waiting to see if anyone picks up on what you've said. At this point, you're not trying to demonstrate your conversational skills. You're trying to build trust with the people in the group.

34. Use small talk to get to big talk.

It's common to hear people say, "I hate small talk." But when you don't know someone, small talk is an ideal place to start. It's like striking a match to light a fire: You need the match, but your goal is to get the fire going.

The key is not to stay with small talk but to use it to ignite deeper, more interesting conversation. There's no time limit on how long that will take, but always have a mindset of going deeper. People who hate small talk are frustrated when the match is lit but there's no attempt to build a fire from it.

That's true when you're trying to enter a group as well. Listen carefully, then start small to see if anything connects. You can "raise the flag" with a comment about the subject they're already discussing. Keep it short, and make sure it's not controversial or opinionated. Your first goal is to build relationships. Once that's done, you've built enough trust to be able to discuss deeper views.

You can also pick up on things in the environment. A logo on a sweatshirt or a unique piece of jewelry can be a starting point for discussion. Look for pictures and decorations in a home or office that indicate a person's values and experiences. Try it right now. Look around you. What are the things you see that you could bring up in conversation?

35. When joining a group conversation, ask, "Am I intruding?"

When you ask if you're intruding, they'll probably invite you to stay, but be sensitive. If they keep talking about something that's obviously of interest only to them, excuse yourself graciously.

If you stay, resist the urge to say too much until you've built trust. It's tempting to try to jump into the conversation with clever or even sarcastic remarks just to show you want to participate, but it's too risky. Keep your comments short and sparse. You're the newcomer to the group, so you want to earn your way in.

Don't begin with comments about jobs, sports, health, politics, or religion. This is not the time to convert someone to your point of view. It's time to make a conversational connection that builds trust.

Think about groups you've been a part of when someone broke in and took the dialogue in a whole new direction. If you were in the middle of a conversation, you were probably frustrated that it ended without warning. Even if no one said anything to the offender, you might have resented them for their lack of sensitivity.

36. Use a few conversational openers to start a conversation.

Use conversational openers that relate to the situation at hand:

- "So how do you know [host or hostess]?"
- "How do you know each other?"
- "Traffic was terrible today. How was it for you?"
- "What brings you here?"

It might feel artificial to have a list of questions to use, but it's a good way to prepare for a conversation. Think of the common ground you have with others and what might be valuable for them, and then craft questions that can open up an opportunity to explore those issues with others.

Be ready for chance encounters. You won't always be the one initiating conversations; others will initiate with you. When they do, your preparation will be your strength. As soon as someone approaches you, anticipate the opportunity to practice what you've learned. You never know when these "accidental" connections can impact your entire future.

CONTINUING A CONVERSATION

37. Be "in the moment" in each conversation.

When there's a lot happening around you, it's easy to get distracted during a conversation with one person. Practice blocking out everything in the background so you can concentrate on the person you're talking to. It shows respect and keeps your focus on the group members instead of yourself.

If the conversation starts to lag, you might lose interest and become more susceptible to the distractions around you. When that happens, the other person will sense that you're disconnecting. Instead, train yourself to see your lagging interest as a trigger, signaling you to stay focused while you bring the conversation to a natural close.

38. Keep the conversation going.

After you've spent some time in a group, you'll probably figure out quickly who you are and are not comfortable with. Or, if you've approached someone directly, you've determined that you want to continue the conversation. It's time to engage that individual.

- Pick up on a comment they made and ask more. People like sharing their opinions.
- Listen for common areas of interest and explore them.
- Whatever they say, follow it up with a clarifying question. It shows you're listening and moves the conversation forward.
- If they express an opinion you disagree with, don't get defensive. Listen carefully to discover what has led them to feel that way. If you don't mind talking about it, say, "That's interesting. I've always felt differently, but I've never heard your perspective before." Don't get into a debate. You need to build trust first. You might win the debate but lose the relationship. They'll get defensive, and it could reinforce their position. They'll find it refreshing if you care about them as a person, not as a project—someone you're trying to convince about something.

39. Smile and make eye contact.

One of the best ways to tell if someone is an introvert or an extrovert is by their facial expressions—especially whether they smile or make eye contact. It's not foolproof, but it's a good indicator:

- Extroverts tend to smile and make good eye contact when they're talking.
- Introverts tend to smile and make good eye contact when they're listening.

Fortunately, you can learn to do both with practice. When people smile (genuinely), it's like an emotional handshake that draws people together. That's because we associate smiling with feeling positive and not smiling with feeling negative. When you smile, others assume you feel positive about them. It can't be contrived, because people sense when it's not real. If you learn to genuinely care about others, they'll pick it up through your smile.

The same is true of eye contact. Most people assume that good eye contact reflects confidence and poor eye contact reflects insecurity or uncertainty. You don't want to stare at someone. That comes across as unnatural. Just practice being intentional about making pupil-to-pupil contact frequently during every conversation.

40. People's names are important to them.

When you meet someone for the first time, introduce yourself and ask for their name. Then use it occasionally during the conversation. If it's an unusual name, ask them to pronounce it until you get it right. They'll appreciate the extra effort.

When appropriate, ask people to spell their names: "Is it S-a-r-a or S-a-r-a-h?" Since their name is important to them, they'll welcome the sensitivity to get it right. When you introduce them to someone else, say, "This is Sarah, with an *h*."

It's a tiny gesture that helps you connect with others because you're showing that you're interested in them as a unique person, not just as somebody you met.

41. Become your own host at every gathering.

If you've had a conversation with one person and you know someone else at the event, introduce the two of them. You've simplified the task for them and started a new group. It also makes it easier to exit when appropriate, since they can keep talking without you.

Each time you talk with someone, make it your goal to find someone to connect them with. Listen carefully to the details they share with you, such as where they live, the ages of their kids, unusual experiences they've had, or odd jobs they had growing up. When you talk to the next person, be intentional about discovering any similarities between the other people you've been conversing with and make the connection.

42. Focus on the other person to keep a conversation going.

So you've made contact, and you have their attention. Now what?

It's common to feel self-conscious at this point. You've initiated a conversation, and the other person is looking you in the eye, waiting for you to say something. By approaching that person, you've implied that this will be a valuable conversation. Now it's time to deliver on your promise. What do you say next?

This is when the adventure begins. You're entering new territory and may be moving out of your comfort zone. But if you take the right tools with you, exploring that territory will produce new insights and topics you've never considered before. The things you need for "conversational survival" will be found as you explore the new ground.

As you enter a new conversation, you might be worried about how you're coming across and what the other person thinks of you. That's natural, but it puts your entire focus on yourself. When the conversation begins, make a conscious decision to move your focus onto them instead. Like an explorer, begin with anticipation of what you'll discover. First, you'll look for those things you have in common. They will create your comfort zone. From that foundation, you're ready to begin exploring the other person's territory. This only happens when you change your mindset from "We won't have anything to talk about" to "We'll find lots of things to talk about."

When I'm teaching a seminar, I make sure I'm set up and ready to go at least an hour ahead of time. That way, as people arrive, I can greet them and begin exploring. It's not a gimmick. I genuinely want to know as much as I can

63

about the people I'll be spending the day with. This helps me because I can tailor my remarks to their specific needs.

But this helps them as well. I've found that when I spend two or three minutes with someone before a class, they don't feel like they're in a seminar anymore. They feel like they have a basic relationship with me. We're no longer in a teacher-listener role; we're two people working together on things that interest both of us. I've often had people comment about the difference those early connections make in their experience.

43. Stay informed.

Planning ahead is the simplest way to feel comfortable in a new conversation. You wouldn't think of building a house without a blueprint. Why enter a conversation without some advance planning? The time you spend thinking through a potential encounter will give you the tools you need to explore any new situation.

Here are some practical ways you can prepare for your next conversation:

- Think about who you might encounter and a couple of things you could say to them. Write them down.
- Determine if there's anything you already know about them: their interests, hobbies, birthday, opinions, or background. Ask someone else who knows them for information. If they have a degree of public exposure, a quick web search could

reveal insights about them. This doesn't mean you're becoming a cyberstalker; you're just finding out as much as you can from public information.

- Read or watch local and national news each day to stay current on the things people might be talking about. My wife and I often ask each other about news stories we've heard or who won key sporting events the previous day. We know that our clients will be talking about those things, and it's helpful to have basic knowledge of current events to be able to participate in those conversations.

- Attend any type of event that stretches you and gives you more things to talk about. Take a free class in something that interests you or join a club. Attend a city council meeting or read through the minutes online to see what's happening in your community. If you're visiting another community, check out the local section of their newspaper online to see what's happening.

For making conversation, it's better to know a little about a lot than to be an expert on one thing. You can dive deeply into that one area but will flounder if the other person doesn't have any common ground with you.

44. Stay focused.

Larry spent his whole career in law enforcement. He once told me that the thing that sets police officers apart from regular citizens is their focus. Most people focus their attention on whatever is in front of them and ignore everything else. Officers are trained to be aware of what's happening in a situation and not be distracted by what's immediately in front of them.

Often, in conversation, we're so caught up in making a good impression that we forget to look at the conversational clues all around us. It's a matter of using all of our senses to listen to, see, and sense the environment. When we're talking, it's easy to focus on what we're going to say next. Good conversationalists observe the little details and use them for direction.

People tell us what they want to talk about. Listen closely and you'll hear snippets of things they're volunteering to explore with you. They're giving you information about the landscape.

When they're responding to a question, listen for things in their answers beyond what was asked. Those are clues about things they are willing to explore. For example, you ask where they grew up. They respond, "Oh, mostly on the East Coast. But since my dad was military, we moved around a lot." You've just been given some clues to form some follow-up questions:

- "What branch of the service was he in?"
- "In what other places did you live?"
- "When you think about growing up, where do you consider home?"
- "How often did you move?"
- "What was it like as a kid having to start your life over every few years?"

45. Stay observant.

A few weeks ago, I spoke in a class at a church in Bakersfield, California. When I met the associate pastor who was in charge of the class, I listened for clues to find common ground. I found out that he was formerly an executive pastor in Phoenix, where I grew up. That led to a brief conversation about sports, since both of us were fans of the Phoenix Suns basketball team. It was a short conversation, but we could have talked about the heat in Phoenix, the price of real estate, or the rapid growth of the city. Those things are common ground for anyone from Phoenix.

Being observant makes it easy to ask questions around areas of common interest.

- At a wedding, ask, "How do you know the bride/ groom?"
- At a conference, ask, "What brought you to this convention?"
- With someone who's recovering from surgery, ask, "Where does it hurt the *least*?" (I used this once with someone, who said it was the most refreshing thing she had been asked.)

46. Give sincere compliments.

A sincere compliment builds a bridge between people and opens up warm communication. It makes them feel good about you for observing, makes them feel good about themselves, and makes them more open to conversation.

Compliment the things you notice that genuinely impress you: their home, decorations, food. Point out things you notice that they do well, such as their ability to talk with clients and guests. And make them feel comfortable and safe in conversation.

There's a fine line between a compliment and flattery. A genuine compliment helps them focus inward, encourages them, and builds their self-confidence; flattery causes them to focus outward and see you as insincere. When you fake sincerity, most people can instantly sense the disconnect, and you've lost credibility.

Never give someone a compliment that you don't mean, and don't use compliments all the time. Even if you're sincere, too many compliments over time can feel like a technique you're using to make them feel better.

47. Practice deep, intentional listening.

When the other person is talking, block out the distractions around you and focus entirely on what they're saying. Try to understand the depth of what they're saying, including their feelings about what they've said. Occasionally restate what they told you in your own words; it shows your interest. This can be done with a comment such as, "So, let me see if I got this straight. You . . ." As you learn about their unique experiences, the door will be open for you to share comments about your own experiences.

There's a balance between focusing on them and talking about yourself. You want to contribute, but you don't want to appear arrogant or monopolize the conversation.

Every healthy conversation involves participation from both people. If it's one-sided, it will be less satisfying over time than if both people get to contribute.

When you talk about yourself, don't dive too deeply. It's one thing to be candid, but avoid sharing too much too soon.

48. Avoid conversational potholes.

Watch out for the conversational potholes that can trip you up in conversation and spoil the encounter. Fortunately, you can learn to recognize and avoid them, creating a much greater chance for a successful connection.

- Don't express controversial opinions right after meeting someone. If they disagree, they'll become defensive. It takes time to build enough trust to share at this level. Build the trust first, and you'll earn the right to be heard.
- Try to avoid talking about work in the early stages of a conversation. It's a natural place to start but focuses on only one dimension of a person's life. Save it for later so that both people can learn about each other outside of their professions.
- Make it a two-sided conversation. Explore the other person's experience, but then contribute from your own.
- Don't tell jokes, even if you think you're good at it. If you don't know someone well, you won't know

what might offend them. Humor, which is simply taking a light view of life, is acceptable. Jokes are too risky.

- Don't pretend you're something you're not. The more integrity you have between your inner and outer self, the stronger the foundation you'll be building for a genuine friendship.

49. Make someone's day brighter.

Last week, I stayed at a hotel in Del Mar, California. As I left my room, a woman from the housekeeping staff was placing newspapers in front of each guest-room door. She was carrying several dozen papers, so I commented that she wouldn't need to exercise that day. She responded with a smile and told me about her one-year-old son whom she picks up throughout the day—her "personal weight-lifting program." As we talked, it was obvious that she wasn't used to hotel guests engaging her in conversation. Entering the elevator, I realized that this short encounter brightened both of our days.

I'm guessing that we were both in a better mood that day because of caring conversation, which carried over to the other people we met throughout our day. By engaging people in genuine, connective conversation, we offer them grace to face the challenges of their lives.

Conversations don't have to be lengthy to be successful. But with a little effort, they can make someone's day brighter—including yours.

50. Serve the other person.

During a conversation, it's natural to be focused on your performance, your appearance, and how the other person is responding. But realize that they're doing the same thing. Most people are thinking of themselves more than the other person. This sounds negative and selfish, but it's realistic. Thinking of yourself is a strategy for personal survival. Recognize that both people are doing it to some degree, and it will minimize the pressure to perform.

When you recognize that reality, it makes it easier to craft a meaningful conversation. The other person is focused on how they're coming across, so you can use that to focus on meeting their needs. Ask open-ended questions, then listen deeply to what they say. Follow up by exploring what they say to get more details. Listen to understand, not just to reply. Make it your goal to serve the other person. After they spend time with you, they should feel better about both of you.

ENDING A CONVERSATION

51. Choose the best time to finish a conversation.

It seems like it would be obvious when a conversation is beginning to drag. But in the middle of the conversation, we might be so focused on keeping it going that we're not thinking about how and when to wrap it up.

If the conversation is going well, we might wait too long to conclude it. Every good, energetic conversation can take a downward turn when you begin to exhaust the topics (or each other). The best time to finish is when things are going well so you'll leave wanting to spend more time together in the future. If you wait too long, you'll end the conversation on a note of low energy. Both of you will think, *OK, that's enough.*

It's better to leave on a high note. Leaving a conversation if you're enjoying it is hard, but you can always come back after making other connections.

It's also valuable to simply be honest. Don't make excuses for why you want to end the conversation. Think about the most interesting parts of your conversation, acknowledge them, and then, making eye contact, use them to make your exit.

Here's an example: "I've never really talked to anyone who has been bungee jumping before. I don't think I'd want to try it, but it's been fascinating hearing your experience. I've got a number of other people I want to connect with before this evening is over, so I need to scoot. Thanks for talking—enjoy your evening." It's gracious and direct, lets them know you valued the conversation, and doesn't leave room for negotiation. You've simply stated what you're going to do and encouraged them along the way.

Ending strong leaves you with a good feeling and helps the other person leave feeling better about themselves. That's when you know a conversation has been successful: You both feel rewarded for the effort.

52. Decide how to escape.

If you find that it's uncomfortable to end a conversation, it might be tied to one of these reasons:

We don't know how to escape without being rude. No matter how badly the conversation may be going, most people hesitate to be rude. So they feel trapped in an uncomfortable situation without the resources to find a way out.

We're afraid of moving on to another conversation. After all, we invested a lot of emotional energy to get the conversation to this point. Why go through that process all over again?

Don't forget that you're trying to develop your conversational skills and explore the rich life experiences of others. If you settle in when you get comfortable, you'll miss the chance to practice your skills and explore other opportunities.

We lose control of a conversation. Occasionally, we connect with someone who uses a conversation for their own therapeutic purposes. Most people ask, "How was your weekend?" The response is typically, "Good. How was yours?" But sometimes people launch into a ten-minute monologue of their entire weekend, including details you really don't want to hear. When that happens, it's difficult to pry yourself away. When people are baring their souls, we don't want to come across as uncaring (even if it's true in that case).

Think through which of these issues might apply to you (as well as others). Decide ahead of time how you'll respond when you notice them taking place so you won't get trapped in a weak ending.

53. Strong endings come from having a clear purpose.

Every conversation has to end sometime. How do you do it gracefully?

The greatest resource you have is *purpose*. If you enter every conversation with a clear sense of where you're headed and what you want to accomplish, you'll have a much greater chance of a fulfilling connection.

It's like a global positioning system (GPS) in your car. You enter the address of your destination. Using data from satellites, the GPS determines your current location and directs you to your destination. If you make a wrong turn, the GPS refigures the route based on your new location. But getting exactly where you want to go is based on having entered the destination.

The same is true with conversation. If you have a clear understanding of your purpose for the conversation, you'll be able to keep the interaction on track when it begins to take a detour. Your purposes might include:

- Meeting new people
- Practicing your conversational skills
- Learning new information
- Networking for business purposes
- Asking for a favor
- Selling a product or service
- Enjoying interaction with other people
- Convincing someone to take a course of action
- Motivating another person to consider an option
- Encouraging someone who needs a lift

Once you have a clear sense of your purpose, you'll find it's easier to choose the appropriate tools and techniques for getting where you want to go.

54. Practice verbal martial arts to steer an uncomfortable conversation.

When I was a kid, judo was the primary form of self-defense that people learned. The appeal was that you didn't have to be strong to defend yourself. If someone was rushing to attack you, you would simply learn to redirect that oncoming energy, and the attacker would end up on the floor. When someone is forcefully moving a conversation along an uncomfortable path, you can redirect that energy into a new direction to take control of the conversation again.

In a coffee shop recently, the person behind me in line was giving me his strong opinions about a story that had been in the news. His forceful approach made me uncomfortable, and I didn't feel equipped to debate his views. Instead, I deflected his comments to go in a new direction: "Yeah, it seems like there are a lot of stories like that on the news lately. When was the last time you saw something on the news that was encouraging instead of depressing?" His tone changed, and he began responding differently without realizing he had been moved in a new direction.

Don't reply directly to a strong opinion or negative comment. Instead, acknowledge their statement and ask a question to steer the conversation in a new direction. It helps you stay in dialogue without letting them set the agenda.

55. End your conversation with grace.

If you've clearly thought through what you want to accomplish before arriving at the event, you can use that as a legitimate tool for exiting a conversation. Use that purpose to tell the person that you're going to do something or talk to someone or be someplace or see something.

For example, "I'm glad we got to connect. I do want to make sure I greet the host before I leave" or "Excuse me, but it looks like Dawn is about to leave, and I need to talk to her about something." The other person sees that you're trying to accomplish something, not just trying to escape them.

If you do that, make sure you do what you said you were going to do. If you excuse yourself to talk to the host, don't get sidetracked along the way by a different conversation. The person you left will notice and see you as dishonest. If you only use it as an excuse but have no intention of talking to the host, you'll find yourself alone. That can start the negative self-talk again, and you'll have trouble initiating another conversation or entering another group.

You can also ask for their help in accomplishing your purpose. At some point in the conversation, let them know what you're trying to accomplish. Ask if they have any expertise in a certain subject or know someone in the room who does. This will give them a sense of partnership as they help you reach your goal.

Here's an example: "Do you know anyone who has started a small business from the ground up? I'm researching that right now and would love to meet someone who has done it." If the person you're talking to knows the subject, you can explore that area more thoroughly. If not, they will be inclined to direct you to someone who might fit that description. If they don't know anyone in that category, you can excuse yourself to continue your search.

56. Take advantage of group dynamics to leave a conversation.

The next time you're at a social function, watch what happens when a small group of people are talking. If one or two people walk up and join the group, one or two others will use that as a chance to move away from that group. There's no clear explanation for their behavior, but you can take advantage of that reality.

Watch the dynamics of the group you're in. When someone joins the group, it's a natural time to slip away unobtrusively. Of course, it won't work if no one joins your group. That's when it's time to utilize one of the other strategies.

Another dynamic is that when someone begins to monopolize a group conversation, people find ways to exit graciously. When you see that happening, make sure you're not the last person to leave. You'll find yourself in an uncomfortable one-on-one conversation that might be hard to escape.

Connecting people is a great way to exit a conversation. If you've already met a couple of people in a social setting, try introducing them to each other. Point out their areas of common interest so they can begin a conversation. They'll appreciate not having to do the hard work of initiating. As they make eye contact and begin connecting, excuse yourself politely and move on.

I use this technique almost daily. As seminar participants arrive, I spend a few minutes getting to know each one. When I find two people who live in the same area, work in the same field, or have something else in common, I introduce them. It's not a manipulative technique. I'm facilitating the flow of conversation by acting as an informal host for the event.

I've found that this is the best way to develop a sense of community in a group. Make sure you do this with the right motives. If you do it simply to get rid of a boring person, the one you introduce them to will resent you for putting them in that situation.

57. Don't make the first conversation a one-time event; build on it for the future.

Hiking in a remote area, you come across a cave. You enter cautiously and begin to explore. Your flashlight reflects off small glassy spots on the wall, so you approach for a closer look. Your investigation reveals that you've discovered a diamond mine. From your experience, you realize how rich that mine is. So you chip out a few stones, put them in your bag, and exit.

An expert looks at the stones and confirms that they are unequaled in quality. Your wealth has increased dramatically. If you return to the mine, you'll increase your wealth immeasurably.

Would you go back? Or would you be satisfied with the diamonds you collected on your first trip?

Obviously, you'd make the return trip. You wouldn't want to leave that kind of potential untouched.

Conversations are like that. We might enjoy the encounter and even discover nuggets of wealth from our time together. But that's often where it ends. Most conversations end when two people quit talking and walk away from each other. But remember you may have a valuable opportunity to mine treasures in that same relationship in the future.

Sales professionals know that it's easier and less costly to retain a current customer than to recruit a new one. That's true in conversations as well; it's easier to build on one you've had than to start a new one. In many cases, following up on a conversation can be an ongoing source of satisfaction and fulfillment for both people involved in the process.

58. Cultivate second conversations.

Extroverts derive their energy from social connections, and they thrive on having a number of people in their lives. For them, it's called networking. They often focus on the conversation they're having with no thought to reconnecting in the future. They're so excited about finding diamonds that they put their energy into finding more diamond mines, pulling a few stones out of each one. They're good at exploring but miss the opportunities that are directly in front of them.

Introverts prefer fewer, deeper relationships. Initiating and holding a conversation is rewarding but drains their energy. By treating each encounter as a one-time event, they're missing the very thing that could make the process less stressful.

Having a second or third conversation provides a number of benefits:

- You don't have to go through the process of starting a new conversation as often.
- You can form deeper relationships with the people you encounter.
- It's nonthreatening because you've already gotten to know the person.
- You're developing a network of people who can introduce you to others.
- In a work environment, you become more visible and influential as you strengthen personal ties.

Regardless of their personality style, most people put their energy into one conversation and ignore the treasure that is available through follow-up. Tapping the potential of repeated connections can lead to a lifetime of satisfying, fulfilling conversation.

59. Be intentional about follow-up to continue a connection.

Think about how connected you feel when someone expresses their appreciation for you. You'll remember their words of affirmation years later. It's human nature to enjoy such encouragement, so offer it honestly in conversation. Find something you admire about their personality, style, or accomplishments and tell them. If your compliment is genuine, it will make the person want to connect with you again in the future.

Focus on the "overlap" between your two circles of life experience. That's where you'll have the greatest chance of connecting again in the future because it's an area of common interest. You're entering their world, and they're entering yours. That overlap begins to grow, which provides fertile ground for further exploration.

Pay close attention to the topics you've discussed to see if there might be an opportunity to build on them later. When the second conversation occurs, make sure you refer to those things.

Listen for hints about their preferred communication style. If they repeatedly mention talking to people on the phone, they'll probably be open to a call from you a few weeks later reminding them of your conversation. If they primarily mention receiving emails, they're letting you know they prefer that you contact them in writing. This may not be your favorite way to connect, but it's theirs. You'll build trust when you use their preferred style to communicate rather than your own.

60. Make a quick, appropriate follow-up to every new conversation.

If someone expresses interest in something you're talking about, offer to get more information to them in a few days. That gives you a valid invitation to make another contact with them. "I'll be glad to get you that information. Would you prefer I bring it by or email it to you?" At the agreed-upon time and place, make the follow-up contact (after preparing for that encounter as well).

If it's appropriate at the end of a conversation, ask directly if they'd like to meet again. Suggest a common-ground activity that you both enjoy. Don't suggest something you haven't talked about, such as bowling or sushi. They might not like either. Keep your suggestion simple. People will be more inclined to meet casually at Starbucks with a new acquaintance than to commit to having dinner or attending a theatrical event.

If they decline, make it easy for them. Don't ask why; just thank them and end the conversation. But send them a short, honest, "It was great to meet you" note the next day, just to keep the connection.

When I'm leading a seminar, participants often ask if they can call me later to talk about the ideas they've heard. As an introvert, I find talking on the phone pretty draining. It's much easier for me to talk with people face-to-face or in writing. I really don't mind responding to emails from these people, because I can edit my responses before sending them as well as control when I take care of them.

Knowing that these invitations will happen, I've prepared a simple, direct response: "I'd love the chance to connect about your questions. Email works best for me. Here's my email address. If you want to drop me a note, I'll be happy to 'chat' electronically." This is a direct, positive response and doesn't leave room for negotiation.

61. Make notes after an important conversation.

If you really had discovered a huge diamond mine, you'd make sure you did everything you could to find it again. In the same way, one of the most important things you can do after a conversation is to find a way to organize your thoughts for follow-up later.

Does that mean making notes? In most cases, yes. Writing down the things you learned while exploring another person's life is one of the best ways to prepare for future conversations.

"But that sounds artificial. If I really cared about the person, I would just remember. I wouldn't have to write stuff down, right?"

Albert Einstein was considered to be one of the smartest men in the world. A reporter once asked him for his phone number. Einstein went to the phone directory, looked it up, and wrote it down. When asked why he didn't know his own number, he replied, "Why should I memorize something when I know where to find it?"[2] He saved his mental energy for more important things.

Most of us have had a detailed conversation with someone and were embarrassed in a later conversation with them when we didn't remember any of it. If we had taken the time to jot a few notes, we could have reviewed them before beginning that second interaction. Note-taking is simply a tool to help us perform an important task. Like any tool, it does certain things better than we can. We use tools to do jobs more easily. It's not a sign of weakness to admit you can't remember details.

62. Organize the information you learn during conversations.

Making notes after a conversation and organizing them might seem fake or manipulative. But trying to remember details takes mental energy. That means that energy is no longer available to work on the task at hand. In fact, research has shown that one of the primary causes of stress is trying to keep everything in your head.[3] If you write something down where it will be available when you need it, you've earned the privilege of forgetting it.

When you know you're going to have a conversation with someone you've spoken with before, a quick review of the key points puts you back on common ground quickly when the conversation begins. They'll be impressed when you remember things they discussed with you before. It demonstrates to them that you paid attention during their initial conversation.

You may ask, "But isn't it dishonest to pretend you remember something when you really had to look it up?" You're not trying to hide your technique. If they ask how you remembered, just tell them the truth. If you took it from your notes, people are just as impressed that you cared enough about their conversation to keep track of what they said.

When I bring up details from a conversation a year earlier, the person usually says, "Wow! Good memory. I'm impressed!" I respond with, "Don't be. I just take good notes." The impact is the same, and the conversation continues on a different level.

THE POWER OF LISTENING

63. Give the gift of listening deeply.

We've all been in conversations where we did most of the talking and the other person did most of the listening. They didn't say much at all, but we walked away thinking, "Wow! That person is a great conversationalist." The encounter stands out in our minds when it occurs because we're not used to it. Listening tends to be a lost art and can be a powerful tool for making connections with others.

When I was a grad-school student in the mid-seventies, a classmate carried out an experiment for a class assignment. He put an ad in the local paper that said, "Will listen without interrupting for one hour. $50." He was hoping to get a few calls from people who would comment on the ad. But before the experiment was over, he made about $600.

A therapist friend calls this "guided listening." Some of his clients are starved to have someone listen to them and are willing to pay for someone to do so in a structured setting.

Few of us learned listening skills as we were growing up. Think about how much time we spent learning to read. The same is true with writing and speaking. We had formal instruction on how to write effectively and had to make presentations in front of a class to develop our speaking skills.

How much formal instruction did you have on how to listen?

For most of us, the answer is none. It's one of the most powerful communication skills, but it hasn't been taught. Someone has said that God gave us two ears and one mouth, which shows the proportion of which we should be using them.

Talk show host Larry King said, "I never learn anything while I'm talking. I realize every morning that nothing I say today will teach me anything, so if I'm going to learn a lot today, I'll have to do it by listening."[4]

64. Check your listening skills.

How do you rate as a listener? When you're in a conversation:

- Do you find yourself planning your reply when the other person is talking?
- Do you tend to interrupt people with your thoughts and reactions before they've finished their thoughts?
- Do you get impatient when someone takes too long to explain something?

- Do you feel more of a need to get your point across than to understand their perspective?
- Do you tend to give advice when people share their struggles with you?
- Do people ever say that you're a good listener?

Your honest answers to these questions can indicate your listening skills. If your answers focus mostly on others, you've learned the value of listening and probably look forward to any suggestions that can help you improve. If your answers focus mostly on yourself, you're on the verge of learning something that could dramatically change the effectiveness of your conversations.

When people feel listened to, they feel comfortable and want to make a connection. When they don't feel listened to, they don't develop trust with that person.

In business, if you don't listen to customers, they'll go somewhere else. They might even pay more for an item somewhere else just because they didn't connect with you. This is especially important in certain professions, such as hairstyling or consulting. People are paying to spend several hours with you and won't repeat the experience if you don't listen.

When someone doesn't listen to us, it feels like they're saying, "I'm not interested in you. I'm more interested in me." That statement might not be accurate, but it's the message that comes across. The person might feel like they're asking the right questions, not interrupting, and doing their best to connect in a conversation. But if we don't feel like they're listening, it doesn't matter.

When we don't feel that the other person is listening, we don't feel a bond with that person. Since trust hasn't developed, we don't feel connected. Without making a connection, the chances of that relationship progressing are pretty slim.

65. Learn how to tell if others are listening.

If everyone had a television monitor on their forehead that displayed exactly what they were thinking, it would be easy to tell when someone had tuned out of a conversation. Since that's not possible, we have to rely on our senses to observe what's happening. Somehow, we just sense when someone isn't listening. What signals do we pick up on that indicate their lack of interest?

Many studies have been done, and the results vary. But all of them point to the same conclusion: When body language and facial expressions don't match what's being said, we tend to believe those physical signals over the verbal ones. One of the earliest studies showed that only 7 percent of communication takes place through our words. Thirty-eight percent comes through the tone of voice, while 55 percent comes through our body language.[5]

We can fake our words, but it's hard to fake body language. When we're talking to someone, we're using our senses to take in information about what's happening. We hear the words, but we're watching their actions. Consciously or unconsciously, we pick up signals that indicate someone isn't listening:

- They don't maintain good eye contact.
- They nod and respond but never engage with the topic or ask for details.
- They respond inappropriately to what you were just discussing (their reply doesn't match the topic).
- Their facial expression is blank.
- Their body language indicates they're not interested in your ideas.
- Their eyes glaze over while you're talking, even while making eye contact.
- They're easily distracted by movements behind you.
- They hear the first few things you bring up and then start telling you what you should do about the situation.

While we might not be conscious of these signals, our subconscious picks them up. The result is that we don't connect with the other person.

If you're not sure someone is listening, ask a question. Then pay careful attention to their answer. If they've been engaged, they'll be able to jump right in with their thoughts. If they've been disengaged, they might appear to scramble to get back on track. At that point, you can decide if it's time to graciously wrap up the conversation or keep it going.

66. Learn to give accurate nonverbal and verbal signals.

As you become more aware of what's happening in your conversations, be intentional about the nonverbal signals you're sending to the person with whom you're talking:

- Learn to consciously tune out everything else that's going on around you. You've probably been around a few people who do that, and it's pretty impressive. It says, "You're so important that the things happening around us don't distract me." It can be tough to do when distractions increase. But practice makes perfect and helps you form a genuine connection with people. If someone calls your name, give them a brief wave to indicate that you'll be with them in a few minutes. Then continue your conversation. If appropriate, you might ask them to join your conversation, which keeps the other person included while helping build their network.
- Nod occasionally to let people know you're listening. You're not necessarily nodding to show agreement. You're acknowledging that you're with them and you're hearing what they're saying.
- Don't interrupt. Usually we interrupt because we think of something we want to drop into the conversation. But if the person isn't finished, they'll feel like you didn't value what they were saying as much as what you wanted to say.
- Don't be afraid of silence. It's like a conversational vacuum; the longer it lasts, the more we feel like

we have to say something. Silence can feel like the breakdown of the conversation is becoming obvious. But if you allow silence long enough to let the other person speak first, they'll give you more information to build on. Salespeople have learned the value of waiting. It allows them to get information they probably couldn't get in any other way.

Make sure your verbal signals are as strong as your nonverbal ones:

- When you're going to add your own comment, relate it to what they've just said. Draw from their perspective and then add your own, which demonstrates the fact that you've heard what they were saying.
- Restate what you've just heard them say. Don't just parrot it; they'll think you're using some psychological gimmick on them. Summarize in your own words what they were just discussing and ask them if you understand it accurately. It takes a significant level of listening to do this so they'll feel understood.

67. If you don't quite get what someone is saying, ask for clarification.

No one wants to appear ignorant, so we tend to pretend we understand when we actually don't. But there's no harm in stopping to ask for clarification.

Author and speaker Kathy Collard Miller has modeled this for me many times. I'll say something to make a point or to make what I mean to be a humorous remark. She smiles and says, "I'm not quite with you. Help me understand." The first few times she did that, I remember thinking how refreshing it was. I wished I could be comfortable enough to do that. But I realized that it displayed a level of confidence in herself to have the security to admit she didn't know everything. In effect, she was saying, "I really want to understand you and need help to make sure that happens." I also realized that it wasn't an advanced technique that I would have to learn; I simply had to do it.

If you don't understand what someone is saying, ask. We're often afraid that if we ask for clarification, they'll think we're not listening. In reality, they'll think the opposite. Taking the time to gain an accurate understanding will reinforce their perception of you as a good listener. That's because you're listening carefully enough to make sure you get it correct.

68. When you catch yourself not listening, admit it and reset.

In the middle of a conversation, you suddenly realize that the other person has stopped talking and is obviously waiting for you to respond. It might be because you were really interested in something they said, and you started thinking about how it applies to you or a situation you have coming up soon or something that happened recently.

If you recognize that you've drifted, don't panic. You probably heard their last few words, so you could pick up on them and simply make a comment about them. But it's easiest to be honest and let them know what happened: "I'm sorry—I missed the last thing you said because I was thinking about what you said just before that. Can I go back there and ask a question?" It's genuine and shows you were listening *so* carefully that your mind wasn't ready to move forward yet.

If you just stopped paying attention, it could be because the conversation has gone long, you're tired, or you have other pressing things on your mind. That's just human, so it's better to admit it than to pretend. "I'm really sorry," you can say. "I didn't sleep well last night, and I just took a fifteen-second mental vacation to the Bahamas. Could you repeat what you just said?"

RETHINKING STRESS

69. Harness the energy of conversational stress.

When we experience the negative impact of stress, we wish we could do away with it. It's hard enough holding a conversation with some people; it's even worse when our body gives off signals we can't control but that seem obvious to others.

But eliminating all stress would make the situation worse. Without stress, we wouldn't have the creative tension that keeps us focused and able to use the best tools and skills we've developed to meet the challenge. Everything we do that's worthwhile takes energy. The right amount of stress channels that energy.

In a social setting, stress often comes from entering unknown conversational territory. You join a group of people in which everyone seems to know each other, and you think you're the only one who feels out of place.

What do we get stressed about in a social situation?

- We're afraid we'll end up alone, with no one to talk to.
- We're afraid we'll be talking with someone and run out of things to say.
- We're worried about the impression we're making.
- We're worried about saying the wrong thing and being embarrassed.

A violin string needs a certain amount of tension to play in tune. Too little and the string produces no sound; too much and the string breaks. Fear of making conversation isn't something to be eliminated. By turning your focus to the other person, you'll feel less stress and you'll be able to harness that energy to make your conversation effective and fulfilling.

70. Change how you think about stress.

The most valuable books and resources about handling stress offer tools for stress *management*, not stress *elimination*. We don't want to totally get rid of stress. We need to learn how to use it to our advantage.

Stress is like gasoline. When a spark hits the fumes, it explodes. If that occurs in your living room, it's devastating. If it occurs in the engine of your car, it gets you where you're going. The gasoline isn't good or bad; the application is what makes the difference.

When stress is controlled, it becomes a powerful tool to use in conversations. The key is to recognize the presence of stress, realize that it's a normal emotion, and harness its power through how we perceive it. As Shakespeare said, "There is nothing either good or bad, but thinking makes it so."[6] We need to evaluate our perception of change.

Hans Selye was one of the early researchers in the field of stress. He studied what stress is, what it does, and how it can be controlled. He suggested that there are two primary types of stress: *distress* and *eustress*. Distress is the bad kind of stress that paralyzes us and keeps us from taking action. Eustress is the good stress that moves us forward when we tap into its energy.[7]

The things that create stress for us are called *stressors*—sources of stress. Interestingly, stressors are almost always neutral. It's what we tell ourselves about the stressor that determines our response to it.

When our kids were teenagers, we often agreed on what time they would come home from an event. A few times, they didn't make it home by that time. That led to a progressive series of thoughts:

- First, we noticed that they were late.
- After a few minutes, we were thinking they were pushing the rules, and we'd have to talk about it when they got home.
- As time passed, we began to feel irritated.
- As more time passed, irritation turned to concern.

- Then we started to worry.
- If enough time passed, we began to panic, imagining the worst.

The later it got, the worse our stress became. But when the door opened a few minutes or hours later, the panic immediately disappeared. (Of course, a new type of stress took over, based on their excuses.)

The simple fact was that they were late. Our stress came from our interpretation of that event. We need to examine and clarify our perceptions.

71. Challenge your negative expectations about how a conversation will go.

If a conversation doesn't feel like it's going well, it's easy to focus on negativity about our skills. That's usually one-sided because we're ignoring the things that are going well. Try these approaches to keep your self-perception from spiraling downward:

- Focus on what the other person is saying instead of how you're feeling. This takes practice, but you'll find freedom when you're not worried about your performance.
- Realize that it might take awhile to get a conversation "working." It's kind of like a slow dance with a stranger; you need time to adjust to their style.
- Be prepared. Know your tools for exploring and how to use them.

- Start small. In a social situation, look for someone who looks friendly and approachable or someone you know. You might observe another person who is like you in some way, such as the way they dress or the fact that they're the only other person at the buffet table trying the liver pâté. Practice your conversational skills with that person.

- Review your "performance after the game"— but *only once*. Sports teams study the films of last week's game to see where they can improve for the next game. There is real value in thinking through what you did well and what you could learn from, as long as you don't focus on the negative.

- Don't compare your performance with that of other people in the room. If you do, you'll probably pick the best conversationalist for comparison, and you'll feel inferior. On the other hand, if you pick the wallflowers, you'll falsely exaggerate your performance. Compare your performance with your own standards—what you've done before and how you want to be in the future.

72. Make the most of your stress.

Stress is a powerful tool for making effective conversation. When we feel stress, it should signal us that something worthwhile is happening. That should trigger us to channel it instead of being paralyzed by it.

Practice taking mental control over the stress. The methods discussed here focus on evaluating situations accurately and truthfully rather than interpreting situations incorrectly. We can visualize a conversation going well. When it does, we should allow ourselves to enjoy the positive feeling that accompanies it. When it doesn't go well, it's uncomfortable. We need to be realistic about what happened, analyzing what we could do differently next time. But then it's time to let it go instead of repeatedly reviewing the things that went wrong.

For example, imagine that you have an upcoming conversation with an important person. If you visualize a negative outcome, stop and ask what's true about the situation. Then you can build the right picture.

We know that people usually want to connect with other people. Visualize that. Picture yourself approaching the person you're meeting. Think about how you'll introduce yourself and imagine the conversation going well. Fix that solidly in your mind. Now you're ready for your meeting. In most cases, you'll find that your positive mental image impacts the success of the actual conversation.

What if the actual conversation doesn't go as well as you'd hoped? Take a few moments to think through what happened. Ask yourself, "If I were in that situation again, what could I have said differently? What would have been a better response to their question?" Now that you've gained some benefit from rehearsing it again in your mind, mentally walk away from it. You're done. Once you've given yourself a quick debrief, move on to the next conversation. Don't allow yourself to get stuck in past conversations that you can't change.

CURIOSITY: YOUR NEVER-ENDING VAULT OF TOPICS

73. Commit to curiosity.

A curious person is usually a good conversationalist. Since they're curious, they like to investigate everything going on around them. That provides them with more potential topics to talk about. It doesn't mean they're an expert on every topic. But conversation becomes easier when we know a little about a lot and a lot about a little.

It's kind of like going into a well-stocked local hardware store. They typically don't have huge quantities of anything, but they always seem to have a few of the exact thing you need. That's OK, since you don't need to buy a lot of one thing.

Imagine a store that sold only nails. That would be great if you needed nails, but you'd be out of luck if you needed plywood. You could have a great conversation with the store owner about nails but nothing else. You wouldn't need to visit that store very often.

The more topics we have in stock on our mental "shelves," the easier it is to start and continue a conversation. We don't have to be an expert in everything. But knowing a little about a lot goes a long way in providing ingredients for conversation. That's why it's valuable to nurture your spirit of curiosity and spark that desire if it's not naturally there.

74. Practice the curiosity of a child.

If you've spent any time around four-year-olds, you know how many times they can ask "Why?" Because of that curiosity, they naturally explore the world around them. Most of that begins with play using blocks, imagination, words, and various objects. Their experience grows in complexity, and they find pleasure in mastering new ideas. Since they enjoy it, they repeat the activity. No one forces them; they do it for the sheer pleasure. That repetition leads to mastery, which leads to a sense of accomplishment and confidence. When they feel confident, they want to keep exploring their world. The cycle begins and ends with curiosity.

As adults, there's a real danger in competence. When we're good at something, we tend to lose our curiosity. After all, what we're doing is working well, so we may not feel a strong drive to challenge the process or do it differently. This lack of curiosity is made worse by the daily challenges of our jobs and things that are constantly changing in our work or home environment. There's so much going on, we look for something that provides routine and stability. That often takes the form of doing what we know how to do well.

There's also a danger in complexity. We recently bought a couple of new appliances for our kitchen. The labels include a strict warning that any repair work needs to be done by a qualified technician, implying that it's beyond the abilities of the owners to try to fix it themselves. It used to be that people would try to repair something first and call a repair shop as a last resort. Today that tends to be reversed; we call for help before investigating.

If you have trouble knowing what to talk about during a conversation, try reviving your curiosity. Listen to what the other person says and go deeper by saying, "Tell me more." Don't use it as a conversational gimmick but to show genuine interest in the backstory of what they're saying. It's an adult version of a child asking "Why?" repeatedly, because you want to know.

75. Learn to see things from a different perspective.

Being good at making conversation is a process. We won't become experts overnight. But a curious mind becomes fertile ground for conversations to grow and bear fruit.

I once heard a photographer from *Arizona Highways* magazine speak, and he was asked what makes his photos so unique. He said that he would look at the same thing other people were seeing, but he would try to figure out what it would look like from a different perspective: from higher or lower, under the light of the setting or rising sun, or on a cloudy day. He used his curiosity to think of different ways to perceive it, which produced a photograph that stood apart in quality. People were amazed at the result because it forced them to look at something they had already seen but from a different perspective.

76. Make curiosity a daily practice.

It's not hard to nurture your curiosity. If you've let yours get a little rusty, a few practical exercises can get it back into shape again:

- Skim the news each day. Read the articles you find interesting, but also glance through a few that stretch you a bit. Read between the lines and look for reasons and motives. You'll be reading the same information others are but seeing something else.

- Look for things around you that you don't normally notice. Take a walk along a busy city street and listen for sounds that aren't human made. Even when you're close to traffic, it's possible to hear a bird sing.

- While walking down a street, try to imagine what's going on in the minds of the people you pass. Watch their facial expressions; try to imagine what their day has been like and where they're headed.

- As you make discoveries, write down what you find. From those observations, develop a list of questions you don't know the answers to. The next time you're in a conversation with someone, bring up a few of those questions to find their perspective.

- When you're watching television, ask the journalism questions (*who*, *what*, *where*, *when*, *how*, and *why*) about the shows. Picture the writers working together to develop a script for the show. Think through a different ending for a drama you've seen.

- Be like a little kid and ask "Why?" repeatedly. Don't use that exact word out loud, over and over in a conversation, but explore the uncharted territory of each conversation. Consciously work to discover things you didn't know when you started.

77. Learn to ask good questions.

Most people assume that the best way to make conversation is to ask a lot of questions. When used properly, good questions can move a conversation forward, giving you an endless supply of material to explore in communication with someone. Using weak questions is like planting a tree in your backyard but using a teaspoon to dig the hole. Weak questions can leave both people frustrated and grind the conversation to a halt. That's why it's critical to use the strongest questions possible for any given situation.

Most people ask questions from their own background and experience. They listen to what the other person says through their own frame of reference, interpreting their conversation through their own filters. Questions are tools for exploring. We use them to find new information in a conversation that wasn't there when the encounter started. A person who is good at making conversation will form their questions from the listener's perspective, not simply from their own experience.

The same applies to everyday conversations with family members and friends. Instead of asking, "How was your day?" say, "Tell me about your day." A simple change in wording can make the difference in the quality and length of the response you receive.

Early in any conversation in a large gathering, ask open-ended questions, like "What brings you here?" "What's your connection with this group?" "How do you know the host?" As you learn about their experience, background, and expertise, pick up on anything that you share in common and pursue it. Maybe you grew up in the same state or had some experience with their company or had the same major in college. The longer the conversation goes, the more common ground you'll discover about each other.

78. Include open-ended questions in your conversations.

For our purposes, we'll divide questions into two categories: *closed-ended questions* and *open-ended questions*.

Closed-ended questions can be answered with one or two words, primarily *yes* or *no*. Used alone, they are ineffective tools for making good conversation. They work best early in a conversation to get things started.

Closed-ended questions aren't bad; they're just limited in what they can accomplish. They're good when you're looking for basic information from someone. If you want to know where someone works, what time it is, or the location of the restroom, a closed-ended question is appropriate: "Where do you work?"

It's like opening a vault inside of which you know there is treasure. The closed-ended questions open the vault. But once you're inside, you want to switch to open-ended questions to mine the treasure.

Open-ended questions are powerful tools for exploring new territory in your attempt to find common ground. They make it difficult to respond with single-word answers and encourage the person to expand their thoughts.

- They make conversation easier for you because you get the other person talking about themselves and their opinions. That person does all the work—you just steer the conversation and listen!
- They make the other person feel safe with you. Open-ended questions allow the person to decide how much or how little they are comfortable sharing. That gives them the feeling that they're in control of the conversation, even though you're steering the flow.

- When people hear a long list of closed-ended questions, which require only quick responses, they feel like they're being interrogated. Open-ended questions keep that from happening since they take longer to answer.
- Good open-ended questions build trust. The other person feels like you genuinely care about them because you're interested in what they have to say. They sense that you listened carefully enough to craft appropriate questions and that you're paying attention to their responses.
- With open-ended questions, you don't have to pretend you know everything; the questions come from your curiosity. That takes the pressure off, allowing you to relax and enjoy the exchange.

Using open-ended questions is like driving a car. The other person does all the work; you just steer. Closed-ended questions are like pushing the car and trying to steer through the window. It takes a lot of work and you won't go very fast. If you do, you'll probably run into something.

79. Learn to use questions effectively.

Open-ended questions can build and maintain momentum during a conversation. For example, someone introduces you to their friend and tells you they spent time in the Middle East. You might start with an open-ended question: "What took you to the Middle East?"

If they respond briefly (e.g., "The military"), you might use a couple of closed-ended questions to get more information and then move back to open-ended ones.

1. "Which branch of the military?" (closed-ended)
2. "How long did you serve? (closed-ended)
3. "What made you choose the navy?" (open-ended)
4. "I think of Iraq as a desert. What does the navy do in the desert?" (open-ended)
5. "What was your time like there?" (open-ended)
6. "What was a typical day like for you?" (open-ended)

Notice that the open-ended questions give the listener the opportunity to expand on the topic. Closed-ended questions require a short answer and don't encourage the person to keep talking:

1. Instead of "Was it hot there?" (closed), ask, "What was the weather like while you were there?" (open)
2. Instead of "Are you planning to go back?" (closed), ask, "What are the things you experienced that would take you back someday?" (open)
3. Instead of "Did you miss your family?" (closed), ask, "What was it like being away from your family for so long?" (open)

As they're responding, listen carefully for new information they offer. Focusing on new information provides options for forming your next question. Think of yourself as a news reporter, asking those six questions that are part of every story: *who, what, where, when, how,* and *why.* Turn those six basic questions into open-ended exploring tools and you'll learn more than you expected about most topics.

If you're genuinely interested in what they're saying, encourage them. A simple statement like "Interesting— tell me more" gives them the incentive to keep talking. Other encouraging responses could include:

1. "I'm not sure I would have handled the situation as well as you did. How did it make you feel?"
2. "What an incredible experience. How has it impacted you since it happened?"
3. "This is exactly the information I was looking for. What else can you tell me?"

80. Refine your questions to keep the conversation on track.

The basic skill of asking questions is pretty straightforward. But in an actual conversation, things can go wrong unexpectedly. When you're asking questions, watch what's happening. If red flags catch your attention, be prepared to adopt some of the following strategies to keep from losing control.

Don't start a conversation with hard or deep questions. The other person might be taken aback by questions that go too deep too soon, and they might feel uncomfortable. Take time to build trust first, and then let the conversation get deeper naturally over time.

When you're using open-ended questions, make sure they're specific enough to focus the conversation. If you ask a question like "So, what do you think about politics?" you'll probably get a limited response. The listener might feel overwhelmed at how much they could say and not even bother to answer. Focused questions give the listener some boundaries to work with, which makes it easier for them to respond.

Only ask questions you really want answers to. The other person will sense if you really don't care, and they'll realize you're just using the questions as a gimmick. The other risk is that they'll take your simple question and give you more information than you ever wanted.

It's OK to write out your questions. To some people, it feels artificial. They assume that if we really cared, we wouldn't need prompting. But there's a lot going on in our minds, and organizing it in an easy-to-remember outline demonstrates that you care enough to take the time to make the biggest impact possible. When I call a CEO, I have my list of questions in front of me. That way I can relax and focus on our conversation, feeling free to explore the new information they provide.

Watch out for risky questions. People's lives change over time, so be careful making assumptions if you haven't seen the person for a while. It could be uncomfortable when you ask about their spouse, their job, or their children only to find out that they're divorced, unemployed, and dealing with wayward kids. You don't know if they're going through painful times or not, so be sure you phrase your questions carefully. Say something like "The last time we talked, you were thinking through some issues related to your job. How did that turn out?" Or "What's the latest with your son?" This type of questioning is honest, since you're not ignoring the obvious issues you both know about. But it approaches the subject cautiously, being sensitive to any issues that might have come up in their life.

The key is to make sure you're really interested in their answer, not just in how good your question is. Listen to their answer rather than thinking about what you're going to say when they're finished.

81. Learn how to answer questions well.

Conversation is a two-way street. Sometimes the conversation goes well without your guidance. The other person is interested in you and begins exploring your experience. You'll recognize it because they're using the same techniques you do.

So, how do you answer questions when they are aimed in your direction?

Honestly. Mark Twain said that you don't need a good memory if you always tell the truth. People respect candor in a conversation, so make sure you speak with integrity. It's the basis for any effective communication.

If you're not sure how to answer, ask a clarifying question. This will give you time to think through a thoughtful response. You don't have to hide what you're doing; just be honest and tell them that you need a minute to think about what they've asked so you can give them an accurate perspective.

Use humor like a scalpel—sparingly and carefully. As mentioned earlier, avoid telling jokes, especially with people you've just met. Just keep a lighthearted view of life and let that come through your conversation.

If you're having trouble reading their response because of little or no facial expression, ask if you've answered their question. You could also say, "Those are my thoughts; what do *you* think?" or "Does that make sense?"

Tell a story to illustrate your position. Make sure the length of the story fits the depth of the question. When you're telling a good story, there's a danger of adding too much detail and boring the other person.

For instance, the person you're talking with mentions having a ficus tree in their yard. You had one and experienced problems with the roots. Telling your story briefly could set up the next topic of discussion: "A ficus tree? Those are beautiful, and we loved the one we had. But we had to cut it down when the roots destroyed our sidewalk. Have you had problems like that?" Notice how you presented your story but kept the emphasis on the other person?

TOUGH CONVERSATIONS

82. Rather than debating when you disagree with someone's position, explore for understanding.

If someone comes to your door to sell you a new vacuum cleaner, you won't have a very good chance of selling them yours instead. No matter how good your intentions are, they're in the selling mindset, which makes it hard to convince them to buy.

When someone strongly disagrees with us or attacks us, there's a natural tendency to defend ourselves and fight back. But you don't want to become adversarial, especially in the first few conversations. If they present an objectionable point, it's usually futile to try to change their mind. If they've brought up the point this early, they're not in the "buying" mindset.

Instead, work to understand their position better. They'll be more open to talking with you, and you'll gain more information about how they think. It doesn't mean you'll end up agreeing with them. But you'll be approaching the conversation with a spirit of humility.

Look at the disagreement as a chance to analyze your position by comparing it with another person's views. Humility means accepting the possibility that your position isn't necessarily perfect. If you stay calm, avoid defensiveness, and listen deeply to what they're saying, you'll have a much clearer view of your position as well as theirs.

Look for areas where you do agree. If you realize that some part of your position is wrong or inaccurate, admit it and apologize. If you need time to think before responding, tell them you're going to do exactly that. It's better to think carefully and email your response than to feel forced into saying something you'll regret.

Possible response: "That's really an interesting way to look at it. I've always believed just the opposite, and you're the first person I've met who feels so strongly about your position. I'd love to hear more about how you reached your perspective."

83. Don't ignore a rude comment; acknowledge it graciously and honestly.

There's no place for rude behavior among adults. As one woman I know says, "They should know better." But sometimes they don't, and it happens anyway. When it does, be careful not to get sucked into their behavior. You don't want to debate with someone who doesn't play fair.

You might feel the need to confront them about their rude behavior. That's difficult to do in the middle of the conflict. If it's a colleague or someone you have to interact with on a regular basis, you might want to plan a gentle approach that's appropriate for their temperament. This could be effective for someone you're close to. But with someone you don't know, it might be ineffective.

A rude person often isn't sensitive to the impact of their words. If you need to say something, give a calm, measured response such as "Ouch!" or "Did you really mean to come across the way you just did?" If it alerts them to their rude behavior and prompts them to change, you've rescued the conversation by making them aware. If not, just excuse yourself and get away. Don't get upset, because that puts them in control. Just express your need to end the conversation and walk away. If possible, join another conversation immediately to get back on a positive note quickly.

84. When someone becomes angry or critical, recognize that there's something deeper happening than what's on the surface.

When a person becomes angry or displays strong emotion, they generally become unable to hear logic. If you try to reason with them, their anger might increase. Make their emotion a trigger to go into listening mode. When you take the time to identify with what they're feeling, you've given them exactly what they need to begin working through the emotion. From that point, they might become open to discussing the issue calmly and logically.

Watch your own emotions. Anger is contagious; make sure you don't catch it.

When someone criticizes you, it feels like they're throwing knives at you. What's the best way to handle that?

- Don't ignore it—you'll get hit.
- Don't pretend it didn't happen—they'll keep throwing.
- Don't excuse their behavior—it doesn't help anybody.
- Don't attack them in return—that's what they're expecting.

Instead, stay calm and explore the source of their criticism. Ask for details so you can accurately evaluate what's being said. There may be parts of the criticism you can agree with. If so, acknowledge them. The easiest thing is to agree with their right to their opinion, even if it's different from yours. Don't spend a lot of energy trying to convince them that they're wrong. When they're sure they're right, they won't welcome input from anyone else at that moment.

Possible response: "I want to understand where you're coming from and why you feel so strongly. Can you fill me in on the specific areas where you have concern about my position?"

85. When someone complains constantly or pressures you to do something, respond simply.

Some people have developed a habit of being pessimistic. They've been that way for so long that they don't just see the glass as half empty—they complain about the size of the glass.

You won't be able to change these people in a single conversation. It's taken them a lifetime of experiences to get that way, so it'll take time to reverse it. In this situation, it's probably best to find a time when you can sit down casually in a neutral situation and ask them questions about how their perspective comes across to others and how it damages their relationships. This won't work if you don't genuinely care about them because they'll sense that you're more concerned about fixing the irritation than you are about your relationship with them.

Occasionally you'll find someone who is committed to changing *your* behavior. Maybe they think you'd be happier if you joined a certain group or changed your hairstyle or bought a pet. Trying to reason with them is usually futile because they've already made up their mind. Instead, be simple and gracious with your response. Say something like "No thanks, I don't want to do that." If they keep pressuring you, don't debate their points. Just repeat that same phrase over and over, no matter what arguments they make. It's a point they really can't refute, and eventually they'll quit asking when they know you're not going to change your answer.

86. When someone talks too much or constantly interrupts, learn to respond directly without coming down on them.

Some people talk incessantly, and you may find it hard to get a word in edgewise. After a while, it becomes a painful effort. So either excuse yourself (they probably won't notice because they're busy talking) or grab something they've said and ask a new question to take them in a new direction. If this doesn't work after a few times, leave. Don't waste your energy.

An occasional interruption is forgivable. But what should you do when it happens repeatedly, when someone interrupts you in the middle of what you're saying and takes the conversation in a whole different direction?

Put up your hand and say, "Hang on—let me finish my thought before we change topics." If it keeps happening, they're not listening and they're more interested in a monologue than a conversation. This may be a signal to move on. Remember the basic difference between a monologue and a dialogue. A monologue takes only one person. Don't feel bad leaving a monologue; you're not needed to make it successful.

If someone walks up and interrupts your current conversation, concentrate and stay focused on your conversation. Acknowledge the newcomer but set boundaries. They shouldn't be able to conversationally steal you away from the other person any more than they should be able to walk up and take food off your plate.

87. When your best efforts don't work in a tough conversation, it's OK to walk away. Just make it your last resort, not your first.

Many of the tough situations we encounter have a common solution: walking away. That doesn't mean you're escaping every situation that is uncomfortable. It means you're making choices about what happens in your conversation. There's no rule that says we have to rescue every conversation that gets strained, especially if we're not the one who messed it up. Fortunately, tough conversations are the exception. When things begin to get rough, analyze what's happening and determine whether the wisest choice is to try to repair it or end it. Walking away is a valid choice when you've determined that continuing wouldn't be in your best interest.

There are no guarantees of success, no matter what you try. You can't control other people's choices; you can only control your own. If someone in a tense situation isn't responding to your attempts to deal graciously and effectively with the issues, you don't have to stay in that conversation. Excuse yourself graciously and walk away. Learn from the encounter and use it as preparation for the next one.

In a gym locker room recently, a controversial news story was on the television. One man reacted by saying, "What a jerk!" He then proceeded to angrily comment on the story and offer his strong opinions of what was being reported. It caught me so off guard that I didn't know what to say, if anything. I walked away wondering how I could have responded. Then I realized that the other person wasn't looking for my opinion; he just wanted to state his.

Handling tough conversations is more of an art form than a science. There's no perfect way to handle those times. But genuinely caring and being prepared are the best tools to feel comfortable and take control when those conversations take place.

ATTITUDE

88. Recognize the importance of attitude in making conversation with others.

Sheila and Tom were driving to a friend's wedding together. They encountered heavy traffic, and Tom became more and more agitated. Sheila tried to convince him to calm down, but that made matters worse. The delay really wasn't anyone's fault; they were just stuck in traffic. She couldn't understand why he was so upset; he couldn't understand how she could remain so calm.

They were both in the same situation. But one of them was upset; the other one wasn't. What made the difference? It all comes down to *attitude*.

It's true that attitude is important. Different people have different responses to the same situation. The situation may be neutral, but their attitude and mindset determine how they feel about it.

That's true in making conversation as well. The right attitude in approaching a conversation can make up for techniques that are less than perfect. We might be concerned about whether we're saying the right thing in the right way and how the other person is responding. But if our attitude is one of genuine caring and understanding, there is a lot more room for less-than-perfect techniques.

89. Develop an attitude of caring for others.

"Can you teach people to care about another person?" That was my question to Jeremy over coffee. He's always been a good sounding board for ideas, and I wanted his input. The question came from research I had been doing for this chapter. Most of what I found focused on how to *appear* to care—what we say, how we say it, and how to subtly manipulate a conversation to make people think we're being genuine. But I found very little about genuine, heartfelt caring.

Jeremy suggested that from his experience, caring isn't something you learn from a book or from someone suggesting that it's a good thing to do. It comes from experiencing it yourself. When you're in a relationship in which someone has genuinely and unconditionally cared about you, it gives you the potential to do the same with someone else. If you haven't experienced that type of genuine caring, you won't recognize it enough to give it to others. "You can't take a person somewhere that you haven't gone yourself," he said.

Caring can't be faked. If we develop the attitude of serving others and meeting their needs, we'll find success in the various conversations we take part in. It takes the focus off us and puts it on others.

Being interested in others is practical wisdom that provides a foundation for making any relationship work. If I put my energy into getting the other person to meet my needs, it forces them to do the same. It sets up a relationship built on selfishness. But if I focus on meeting the other person's needs above my own and they do the same, we can base the relationship on a spirit of giving rather than taking. That builds long-term trust and powerful relationships.

90. Remember that you can't control someone else; you can only control yourself—your attitude and choices.

On a trip to Ethiopia several years ago, I was uncertain about communicating with people there since I wasn't familiar with the Amharic language. During the flight, I learned a few useful words and phrases in the Amharic language from my friend Steve, who had been there many times before. The people we would be working with spoke enough English to hold a simple conversation, but I felt it would be a little embarrassing to consider dropping in my elementary phrases in their language. Upon arrival, I found that they appreciated my shaky efforts because they knew I was trying to connect. They chuckled at my pronunciation, but we formed a quick bond because they knew I was reaching out to them.

Not making those kinds of attempts can seem arrogant to them. It's as if we're saying, "I don't need to make things easier for you, and I'm not even going to bother to try.

You need to communicate in my language to make things easier for me."

I can't force you to like me, take interest in me, or meet my needs. You are free to choose how you feel and how you act toward me. The more I try to make you do anything, the more frustrated I'll be when you don't cooperate.

The only thing I have control over is my own choices. I can choose what I say to you, how I act toward you, and how I feel about you. I can choose to meet your needs. You can't force me to do that; it's a choice I have to make.

So what *can* I do? I can't control you, but I can influence you. The choices I make will influence the choices you make. If I choose to meet your needs, that will have an influence on the choices you make.

So, what are the basic needs people have? To be *known* and *appreciated*. Being known means that people have taken the time to focus on us, investing their energy in our lives. They recognize that we exist and interact with us on that basis. Being *appreciated* means that they like us and demonstrate that connection.

91. To change your attitude, change your thoughts—which will eventually change your actions.

The way we think determines who we are, since our thoughts lead to our attitude. That's why our attitude is so important: It shows what's really going on inside. In turn, our attitude determines our actions and choices.

Our *thoughts* lead to our *attitude*, which leads to our *actions*.

We were born with our own unique personality. The key to success isn't to change that uniqueness; it's to learn to accept it and celebrate it. Once we get a clear picture of who we are and our distinct characteristics, we're able to develop that unique design to impact others.

Our self-talk is powerful. What we believe about ourselves directly impacts our ability to connect with others. If we see ourselves through a negative lens, we'll assume that other people are seeing us that way too (and it will change the way we talk to them). If we see ourselves through a realistic, positive lens, we'll assume that others see us that way as well. That's why it's important to see ourselves accurately.

92. Nurture an attitude of gratefulness and contentment.

The goal of making conversation is to make a connection, not to get the other person to write you into their will.

Anytime you compare yourself with someone else, you're going to see yourself unrealistically. The key is to recognize your uniqueness, embrace it, and run with it. When you do that, you'll have a positive outlook that comes from within. That in turn will attract others.

Everyone seems to be busy, so time is a valuable commodity. When someone spends time talking with you, they're giving you a valuable gift. Recognizing how much it means that they give you their time will change the way you interact with that person.

Even if they're not the perfect conversational partner, you're receiving something no one else has at that moment: their attention. Enjoy it—don't always be mentally rushing toward the next conversation.

Develop an attitude of contentment, which includes embracing who you are and what you're about. It's a peaceful recognition that we're not performing for others; we're sharing part of ourselves with another person, and they're doing the same. The result can be a satisfying contact in which both people have given of themselves.

HIGH-TECH TALKING

93. Use technology as a tool to enhance conversations, not to replace them.

In the twenty-first century, email, social media, cell phones, and internet communication have become the norm. Carrying a mobile device enables people to communicate silently in the middle of a meeting without disturbing anyone around them. It seems efficient, since a person can begin and end a conversation with someone without ever leaving a meeting or event. But efficiency is different from effectiveness.

Technology is part of our culture, and we need to learn how to effectively balance electronic and live conversations. Even though we're able to respond quickly, doing so might be taking us away from more important tasks and conversations. We focus on *efficiency* (doing things right) instead of *effectiveness* (doing the right things), putting activity ahead of results.

Smartphones have made it much easier to connect with people quickly. Voice mail allows us to leave messages, and texting puts people in touch instantly. The list of advantages is long, and we wonder what we ever did without these tools. But that convenience doesn't mean our communication is better.

On the phone, people can't see our facial expressions or body language. So it can be hard to get a clear picture of how the other person is responding. In this book, we're trying to make conversation easier, not harder. Not having those visual clues available can really make the process tougher than it needs to be. Email and texting remove verbal clues as well.

The basic principles of making conversation still apply in electronic communication. We still have to deal with apprehension, approach people, and follow the rules of politeness and etiquette. Technology presents some unique challenges in those areas, and there are things to watch out for or do differently. No matter how we do it, the goal is the same: to communicate, connect, and converse with another person.

Communication is genuine connection between two people. Technology can help but will not replace that connection.

94. Know the advantages and disadvantages of digital communication.

There are many advantages of digital communication:

- It's a simple way to stay in touch with more people in less time more often.

- Email can be written and read at any hour of the day since time zones are not an issue.
- The delivery is immediate, anywhere in the world.
- The reader doesn't have to take notes on what you've said since it's all in writing. Unlike a paper document, the recipient can copy and paste any section to forward or use in another document.
- Some people express themselves better in writing, so it's a good way to accurately express thoughts and feelings.
- You can often directly reach people you wouldn't normally have access to, such as the CEO of an organization.

For many people, these advantages outweigh the disadvantages. Email has become not only an accepted form of communication but an expected one as well.

That doesn't minimize the disadvantages:

- You can't see the other person's body language or facial expressions, which make up 93 percent of how they communicate.
- It's easy to misread someone's meaning based solely on their choice of words.
- Since it's efficient, there could be a tendency to rely on this form of communication and avoid having live conversations. For a shy person, it can make their conversational skills even worse. The better they become online, the less incentive

they have to force themselves out to practice in person.

- In writing, people can pretend to be something they're not, because you're not there to see their visual cues.
- Whatever you write casually is permanent and can be distributed widely.

These disadvantages can be particularly troublesome for quiet communicators because they eliminate the non-verbal cues that make it easier to read people's reactions during a conversation. The key is balancing the use of email with other forms of connection.

95. Treat digital conversations with the same care as in-person conversations.

For all of its benefits, email has some potentially painful outcomes that can be easily avoided with these reminders:

- Always check one last time that you're sending the right message to the right person. It's painful to have to do damage control after the fact.
- Be careful using abbreviations. They're commonly used in emails, but you could run into problems if the recipient doesn't understand them.
- Be careful not to hit "Reply All" when you want to reply only to the individual who wrote the email. You might find your personal discussion in the hands of dozens of other people.

- Don't give lengthy emails about your opinions without the recipient's permission. You might be imposing when they would rather not spend time on that topic.

- For special events, avoid using digital notes. An event like a wedding deserves a mailed card in most cases, and thank-you notes have more impact when they're handwritten and mailed. You'll stand out in your communication with the other person when they're inundated with emails.

- Keep business emails business and personal emails personal in the early stages of a relationship. Don't cross the line by making a business email chatty if you haven't developed a friendship that warrants it.

- When sending an email to a group, make sure you hide (BCC) their email addresses. I know the email addresses of several celebrities because someone who knew both of us simply inserted our names and email addresses in the address line. Any recipient on the list can see all of the other recipients and their addresses, which could feel like a breach of trust for some individuals.

- Avoid most types of humor in emails. Humor involves tone of voice, timing, and facial expressions to be effective. Those are missing in an email, so the chances of it succeeding are almost nonexistent.

FINE-TUNING YOUR SKILLS

96. Avoid conversation killers.

- Don't ignore someone else's feelings. We might assume that if we don't acknowledge someone's feelings or if we minimize them, those feelings will simply disappear—but it usually makes the situation worse. Use listening skills to identify with what the other person is feeling and offer support, which builds trust.

- When someone is upset, don't try to fix them. Strong emotion needs to be felt, not swept under the rug.

- Don't let your mind wander when it takes someone a long time to get to the point. Recognize that it's happening and concentrate on what is being said. Make sure you don't jump ahead, filling in the blanks when they have too many pauses.

They'll feel rushed and think you're anxious to get out of the conversation.

- Don't assume that your initial impression of a person is accurate. The longer we talk with someone, the more we learn what's under the surface. We should assume that no matter whom we're talking to, what we're hearing and seeing isn't the whole story.

- When you tell stories about your life, make sure they're accurate. You never know when someone you're talking with was at the same event and knows that you're embellishing the details. From that point on, they'll question your integrity.

- Don't give unsolicited advice. (It comes across as arrogance.)

- Don't correct people (their story details, their grammar, or their conclusions). It's more important to be caring than correct.

- Don't gossip to others after a conversation. (They'll assume you'll be talking about them with the next person.)

- Don't finish people's sentences for them. (That's their job, not yours.)

97. Practice the things that nurture connection.

- Listen carefully to what the other person is saying and feeling before presenting your position. We tend to rush in with our perspective, telling them how they should feel or what they should do. But when we reply before deeply listening to them, our ideas might not even be heard. If we give unwanted advice when we haven't listened, we're implying that they can't handle the situation on their own.

- Make it your goal in each conversation to discover something you didn't already know about the other person, no matter how long you've been friends.

- Almost everyone has knowledge or experience we don't know about. Make it a point to find out as you explore each conversation.

- Use the Golden Rule: "Do unto others as you would have them do unto you." Think about the things people do in a conversation that you find rewarding and practice those same things with them.

- At the beginning of a conversation, assume that you've been asked to repeat what you've heard to your spouse or friend at a later time. You'll listen better and retain more information since you'll be responsible for re-creating the discussion points accurately.

- Decide that you genuinely want to listen. You can't fake it. Somehow that disinterest will come through your body language or facial expressions.

- As you're listening, remember that what the other person is saying is being filtered through their life experience and perspectives. So while you think you understand, recognize that there might be a different or deeper meaning than you initially thought.

98. You're only responsible for your side of the conversation, not how the other person responds.

Your job is to handle your side of the conversation, practicing and perfecting your technique and approach. You're not responsible for how the other person responds, so don't let it define your perspective. You won't connect perfectly with everyone because no one is perfect.

It's kind of like shopping for produce. When you enter a grocery store, you head for the fruits and vegetables. They're probably all good for you, but you like some more than others. You'll look at them all but end up selecting which ones you want to take home. Just because you don't buy them all doesn't mean you're a poor shopper. You're simply choosing which ones meet your own needs.

We're not shopping for conversational partners. But as we engage a variety of people in conversations, we'll choose which ones we want to continue connecting with while enjoying our brief time with others.

Be realistic. Start slow, monitor your progress, and enjoy the ride. Work in your comfort zone, but gradually push the boundaries. Over time, your comfort zone will grow.

You can be comfortable and confident in conversations, but you don't want to totally eliminate the creative tension that makes for a good interaction. There's no such thing as a casual conversation. Anything worthwhile takes effort, but you'll be operating from a position of confidence.

99. Use an accurate mindset to build your conversational skills.

Be careful not to have a mindset that sees the process as harder than it actually is. Like any worthwhile skill that you don't know, it seems hard when you're at the bottom of the learning curve. But if you learn to explore gradually and practice your new skills, you'll be able to talk to anyone, anywhere. You won't have to be intimidated by those conversations because, like any other skill, you've learned what to do when it occurs.

Zig Ziglar often said that if you help everyone you meet get what they need, you'll get what you need in the process. That's why you want to focus on others instead of yourself. If you focus on your performance, you'll never feel the fulfillment that comes from healthy relationships. But if you learn to focus on the other person, personal fulfillment will be a fringe benefit.

When you're in a social situation and you're wondering whether you should approach a certain person to initiate a conversation, listen carefully to your self-talk. You'll probably find that you're evaluating what the other person will be thinking if you approach them. If you feel they'll have a negative opinion of you when you walk up to them, ask yourself what is causing that assumption. Is it something in their body language or facial expression? Or are you simply projecting your own fear onto them, anticipating a negative reaction?

Ask yourself, "What is the worst possible thing that could happen?" Then go for it. See how close the reality matches your assumption. In the majority of cases, you'll be pleasantly surprised. After the conversation, make sure you consciously compare how it turned out with how you expected it to turn out. You'll find that most people will respond positively when you approach them with genuine interest.

Keep your conversations positive, since that sets the tone for future conversations. If the other person enjoyed their time with you, they'll have a positive feeling when you meet again in the future. They'll remember how you made them feel the first time, and they'll look forward to feeling that way again. Relax and enjoy the process. Stay lighthearted; don't take yourself too seriously.

100. Remember that the best conversationalists didn't start that way. They learned how, and you can too.

It always amazes me to watch top athletes—how they can put the ball almost exactly where they want it to go. I once watched a pro golfer hit the ball past the green on a slope. It rolled back to within inches of the cup. And he did it on purpose.

That's why people enjoy watching the Olympics. You get to see world-class athletes do things that boggle the mind.

There is one important thing to remember as we watch these gifted athletes: *They weren't always that good.* They reached elite levels because they did what they were gifted to do and practiced to hone their skills.

Not everyone will become a world-class conversationalist. But that's OK. Just because you can't play golf like the top pros doesn't mean you can't play well and enjoy the game. In the same way, anyone can practice the skills of conversation to become confident in any situation.

Rick Warren suggests that everyone has a purpose that involves impacting the lives of others. When our conversational skills help us build relationships, we have the opportunity to impact our world. That's why Mother Teresa said her mission was "to be a pencil in the hand of God."[8]

In a world of fast-paced electronic communication, there is an even greater need for face-to-face interaction. People's lives are changed through heart-to-heart conversation, not efficient emails.

Spend time developing your conversational skills and you'll see steady improvement. That in turn will help you achieve all the things you want to accomplish in life. Want to touch the lives of others? Making conversation is the basis of making it happen.

A FINAL WORD

No matter what your personality style, you can make conversing one of the most rewarding and positive things you can do in life. Since you don't have a choice (we have to make conversation to make it through life), you have every motivation to take the steps to get really good at it. By consciously working on your skills, you'll be able to enjoy connections you already have and look forward to new conversations. You can build your skills at a safe, comfortable speed, using methods that fit your style and moving into new skill levels when you've mastered the current ones.

One phone company used to have a slogan that said, "Reach out and touch someone." Take that challenge. Be yourself, develop your skills within your own unique personality, and reach out to others. You'll find yourself on a journey that can change your life—and impact the lives of everyone you meet!

ACKNOWLEDGMENTS

This is a short book, especially compared to my previous ones. So it feels like this section should be short as well. That's not hard to do, because there are a few people who show up in this section every time:

- My wife, Diane, who has been my cheerleader and strategist for the past forty-five years. She has read every word I've written, made suggestions that took me out of my own head, and made every-thing richer. And without her amazing influence in my life, none of these words would be in print.
- My kids (and kids-in-law), who have always asked the uncomfortable questions and told me plainly what I needed to hear. They're a gift and are the most important people in my life (next to Diane).
- My grandkids, who are unimpressed by the fact that I write a bunch of books but skim each one thoroughly to see what stories I've told about them (and there are plenty).

- Dr. Vicki Crumpton, who has edited every word I've ever written in these books. It's like taking a master class in effective writing, and I'm spoiled that she's been the only editor I've ever had. She knows how to keep my voice in my books but still make sure you're able to make sense of them.

I could add individuals who have been a part of all my books, but there's one big category of people that is represented in all of my writing, including this book: *everyone I've ever connected with.* My ideas come from the thousands of conversations I've had over the years, providing the building materials to shape concepts. I have several friends who hesitate to talk to me, saying, "If I tell you what I've been doing, it'll end up in one of your books."

That's true. And for that I'm grateful.

Thanks for the role you play in my life, no matter who you are. You make all this stuff possible.

Let's keep it up, OK?

NOTES

1. Rick Warren, *The Purpose Driven Life* (Grand Rapids: Zondervan, 2002), 17.

2. Phillip Lee Edwards' Favorite Quotes, "A Wise Man," https://sites.google.com/site/philledwardsauthor/favoritequotes.

3. Sean Merritt, "This One Thing That Will Help with Mind Wandering and Stress—Writing Things Down," Medium, May 30, 2018, https://medium.com/betterism/this-one-thing-that-will-help-with-mind-wandering-and-stress-writing-things-down-2df30276d590.

4. Larry King, *How to Talk to Anyone, Anytime, Anywhere* (New York: Random House, 1994), 40.

5. Albert Mehrabian, *Silent Messages: Implicit Communication of Emotions and Attitudes* (Belmont, CA: Wadsworth, 1980), 75.

6. William Shakespeare, *Hamlet*, act 2, scene 2.

7. Hans Selye, *Stress without Distress* (New York: NAL Penguin, 1974).

8. Edward W. Desmond, "Interview with Mother Teresa: A Pencil in the Hand of God," *Time*, December 4, 1989.

Dr. Mike Bechtle (EdD, Arizona State University) is the author of seven books, including *People Can't Drive You Crazy If You Don't Give Them the Keys*, *Dealing with the Elephant in the Room*, and *It's Better to Bite Your Tongue Than Eat Your Words*. His articles have appeared in publications such as *Writer's Digest*, *Focus on the Family*, and *Entrepreneur*. A frequent speaker, Bechtle lives in California. Learn more at www.mikebechtle.com.

FOR MORE
COMMUNICATION TOOLS,
PRACTICAL INSIGHT,
AND MOTIVATION, VISIT

MIKEBECHTLE.COM
🐦 📷 **@MIKEBECHTLE**

Discover More
Resources from Mike